Susan Baltrus

Contemporary Books

Chicago   New York   San Francisco   Lisbon   London   Madrid   Mexico City
Milan   New Delhi   San Juan   Seoul   Singapore   Sydney   Toronto

Library of Congress Cataloging-in-Publication Data

Baltrus, Susan.
    Thinking games for preschoolers / Susan Baltrus.
        p. cm.
    Includes index.
    ISBN 0-7373-0356-5
        1. Education, Preschool—Activity programs. 2. Thought and thinking—
Study and teaching (Preschool) 3. Education, Preschool—Parent participation.
I. Title.
LB1140.35.C74 B35 2001
372.13—dc21

                                                     00-053462

Contemporary Books

A Division of The **McGraw-Hill** Companies

0 1 2 3 4 5 6 7 8 9 DOH/DOH 9 8 7 6 5 4 3 2 1 0

International Standard Book Number: 0-7373-0356-5

This book was set in ITC Legacy Serif by Carolyn Wendt.
Printed and bound by R. R. Donnelley & Sons Co.

McGraw-Hill books are available at special quantity discounts to use as
premiums and sales promotions, or for use in corporate training programs.
For more information, please write to the Director of Special Sales,
Professional Publishing, McGraw-Hill, Two Penn Plaza, New York, NY
10121-2298. Or contact your local bookstore.

ACKNOWLEDGMENTS

I am grateful to the dozens of creative parents and educators who shared their innovative ideas for thinking games with me. A special thanks is due to Michael Baltrus, Cynthia Baratta, Mario Baratta, Kathy Beam, Joni Bloom, Mark Bohn, Kristen Diebus, Elizabeth Emhardt, Nadine Evans, Alexandra Flatley, Joseph Flatley, Michaela Flatley, Robert Goretti, Mary Guirleo, Jennifer D. Harnish, Trish Homer, Pat Johansen, Kate Merrigan, Amy Paxson, Marion Pope, Brahm Rockwood, Susan Rockwood, and Louise Tharrett.

To Lauren, Sam, and Jillian

CONTENTS

HOME GAMES 43

OUTDOOR GAMES 141

INTRODUCTION

Preschoolers are acutely aware of the world around them. They generate endless questions as their inquisitive minds soak up every drop of information available. As parents, it's gratifying to watch as our preschoolers grasp new concepts, learn how to express themselves, and develop problem-solving skills.

MAKING EVERY MINUTE COUNT

We want to make the most of the time spent with our children. But we spend so much of our time completing life's daily tasks—driving in the car, straightening up the house, making dinner, waiting at the pediatrician's office, getting dressed, and so on—we don't seem to have enough quality time with our children.

We also worry: Are we giving our children an adequate foundation for learning? What can we do to help them grow and learn? How can we help them become more verbal? How can we teach them to be better problem solvers? Can we introduce skills now that will help them later on? How can we nurture their creativity? How can we encourage them to use their imagination? How can we build their self-esteem? How can we teach them to have a positive attitude toward learning? What can we do to strengthen our relationship with our children?

Thinking Games for Preschoolers is jam-packed with fun and stimulating games that create opportunities for on-the-spot learning. The games in this book show children that learning can be fun and build an appreciation for activities that challenge young minds.

WHY GAMES?

Some parents may be hesitant to play structured thinking games, preferring conversation, solving simple math problems, or reading books with their children. But when conversation runs dry, or when the family has a long road trip ahead, or when math problems become boring, playing thinking games can be fun and energizing, and they open up a whole new world—the world of games.

The thinking games presented in this book vary from loose and unstructured activities to competitive games with rules and points in an effort to offer something for every parenting style. There are games that involve math, storytelling, imagination, words and language, memory, music, and physical participation. Each game stimulates a different set of skills or thought processes.

HOW PRESCHOOL CHILDREN THINK

Preschoolers use many different types of thought processes, and they use all their senses—sight, sound, smell, taste, and touch—to gather information. They use problem-solving skills to count, measure, sequence, and categorize. They test the world around them through experimentation. They think about how things fit together, and they use their imagination for fantasy play. They use language, nonverbal communication, and art to express themselves. Finally, they use their motor skills for such activities as cutting with scissors or jumping rope. Playing different games stimulates these various thought processes.

In this book, these thought processes are grouped into ten categories. Each game stimulates one or more of the following thought categories, which are described in each activity's "Purpose" and "Skills Developed" section. (The Game Overviews section recaps these skills. Games are also indexed by thought category.)

1. **VISUAL OBSERVATION:** Games that help children gather information visually, become more aware of their surroundings, and relate abstract concepts to the real world.

2. **PROBLEM SOLVING:** Games that require critical thinking to count, measure, order, and categorize.

3. **EXPERIMENTATION:** Games that allow children to test the world around them through experiments and to draw conclusions. Children can ask "what if?" questions and try to answer them.

4. **AUDITORY AND OTHER NONVISUAL OBSERVATION:** Games that allow children to gather information through hearing, smelling, tasting, and feeling.

5. **MEMORY:** Games that develop short-term memory.

6. **SPATIAL ABILITY:** Games that explore spatial relationships and show how things fit together.

7. **IMAGINATION:** Games that emphasize creative thinking and imagination.

8. **LANGUAGE AND EXPRESSION:** Games that help build strong communication skills and an understanding of word sounds.

9. **ARTISTIC EXPRESSION:** Games that encourage self-expression through art.

10. **MOTOR SKILLS:** Games that utilize fine and gross motor skills.

HOW THESE GAMES WERE DEVELOPED

I relied on my roles as a researcher, parent, teacher, and writer to compile this collection of thinking games. Dozens of creative parents and educators generously contributed their ideas based on their own experiences. This collection was generated from a broad range of talented individuals in order to appeal to a broad range of children and parents.

Many of the parents I interviewed for this book told me that they often played the same two or three games with their preschoolers.

They thought these games were not unique, but this couldn't have been further from the truth. Surprisingly, I encountered few duplicates. So wide is the range of thinking games parents play with their children that I was able to collect nearly one hundred great game ideas.

THE VALUE OF GAMES

First and foremost, the games in this book are designed to be entertaining. If thinking games aren't fun, kids will undoubtedly get bored and resist playing them. Equating learning with fun is the most valuable lesson this book has to offer. The games are also designed to be enjoyable for parents, too, because it's important for adults to be engaged and interested in the activities.

Second, the games are varied. Each of the ten thought categories listed above is represented. Some games focus on a couple of the thought categories, and others use several. To stimulate all kinds of thinking, try to play games from each of the categories.

Third, these games are easy to play. They require little or no preparation. You can use materials and supplies you probably have at home. Many don't require any materials and can be used for on-the-spot learning.

Fourth, these games will last. Parents of older children told me they started playing some of these games when their children were preschool age, and their children still enjoy playing them at ages eight, ten, and twelve. Many offer suggestions for making the games more challenging as kids get older.

Finally, playing these games adds a new dimension to your relationship with your child. They open up new lines of communication and show your child that you care.

Aside from stimulating thought and encouraging fun, games bring another benefit to young children. Playing games teaches preschoolers about rules, taking turns, and group play. Games that are noncompetitive build a foundation for good sportsmanship because children learn that the fun is in *playing* the game, not in *winning* the game. Games also help develop cooperation, negotiation, and social skills as children play in a group.

A WORD ABOUT WINNING

Most preschoolers are not gracious losers. They love to play competitive games, and of course, they love to win, but losing can be a frustrating experience and may result in withdrawal or reluctance to play future games.

Competition, however, can transform an activity into a game. For example, driving with your child in the car and pointing out familiar street signs is an *activity*. But challenging Alyson to identify all the yellow street signs and Ben to identify all the red street signs changes the activity to a *game*. Which version would be more engaging to preschoolers? Probably the game version. But playing games doesn't mean that winners and losers must be declared. It's not necessary to keep track of how many yellow signs Alyson spots and how many red signs Ben spots. If the children do keep score, don't compare Alyson's six points to Ben's eight when you reach your destination. Focus on the value of the counting lesson rather than on winning and losing.

WHEN ARE CHILDREN READY?

The games in this book are intended for preschool children, roughly defined as kids ages three to six. You may find that some of the games are too advanced for three-year-olds or too simple for six-year-olds. If your child is not ready for a particular game, wait six months, then try again. Most of the games are fun for children who are six or older.

All the games can be played with children who have not yet learned to read, and many stimulate and exercise prereading skills. Once your child learns to read and write, you may incorporate the enhancements described to make many of the games more challenging.

HOW TO USE THIS BOOK

Thinking Games for Preschoolers is organized into four main sections:

1. Car Games
2. Home Games
3. Outdoor Games
4. On-the-Go Games, which can be played while you're doing something else, such as waiting at the doctor's office, going grocery shopping, or riding in an airplane or on a train.

Many games overlap into other categories, so the four sections should be considered as loose guidelines. For example, many games in On-the-Go can be played successfully at home, too. And many of the Car Games are also great On-the-Go Games.

For each game, you'll find a detailed description of its purpose, a list of the materials (if any), the number of players, how to play, an example of how one family played the game, hints and variations, and a discussion of the skills developed by playing the game.

The Game Overviews section offers a brief description of each game and summarizes the specific skills enhanced. This is a handy reference guide after you've perused the games in the book, or it may help direct you to the games you'd like to read more about.

Regard these game descriptions as a starting point. You and your children may want to modify the games or use them as inspiration for new games. Encourage your children to question the methods and to make suggestions for improvements. Soon they'll be inventing their own games!

When you're playing thinking games with your children, remember these pointers to keep the learning process fun.

- **BE POSITIVE.** Encourage your children, praise their efforts, celebrate their successes, and build their self-esteem.
- **BE FUNNY.** Use your sense of humor. Preschool children love silliness!
- **BE ENTHUSIASTIC.** Enjoy yourself, and your spirit will be contagious.
- **BE PATIENT.** Children may not grasp the games at first. Not every game is right for every child.
- **BE REALISTIC.** The attention span of preschoolers is very short. Don't expect any one game to last more than a few minutes. Be ready with another one!
- **BE FLEXIBLE.** Take your cues from your children and be willing to switch gears, change the rules, or respond positively to any other suggestions they may have.

CAR
GAMES

HIPPOPOTAMUS

PURPOSE: To exercise listening skills, critical thinking, imagination, and verbal communication skills.

MATERIALS NEEDED: None

NUMBER OF PLAYERS: 2 or more

HOW TO PLAY: The first player thinks of a sentence that describes a true fact about one or more of the other players. The player says the sentence aloud, but substitutes the word *hippopotamus* for one of the nouns. Other players try to guess the correct word. The first player to name the correct word thinks of another sentence.

EXAMPLE: Lauren says, "Mom brought her *hippopotamus* to work this morning because she thought it might rain." Sam correctly guesses *umbrella*, so he creates the next sentence.

HINTS AND VARIATIONS
- Use the word *hippopotamus* to create silly sentences.
- Adult players may need to give a few examples before preschool players are able to construct their own sentences.
- Once your child has mastered this game, try substituting *hippopotamus* for other types of words, such as verbs.
- Instead of using *hippopotamus*, use your child's name.

SKILLS DEVELOPED: As your child listens to your sentences, she sharpens listening skills and uses critical thinking to determine the correct word. She's likely to find the role of creating her own sentences to be more challenging, but more rewarding (and funny!). This part of the game develops imagination and verbal communication skills.

PEOPLE STORIES

PURPOSE: To use visual observation, imagination, and language to create and tell stories.

MATERIALS NEEDED: None

NUMBER OF PLAYERS: 2 or more

HOW TO PLAY: While riding in the car, the youngest player points out a person outside (someone walking, riding in another car, or appearing on a billboard). He begins to create a story about that stranger. The next person picks up where the first player left off, adding details. The storytelling goes back and forth, each player adding a sentence or two to continue the story. The story can continue until it reaches a natural conclusion or until the ideas run dry. Another player selects a new stranger, and the storytelling begins all over again.

EXAMPLE: Keith points out a woman who is standing on the sidewalk and holding a large bag. He begins, "That woman's name is Rachel. Today she went shopping and that's why she is holding a large bag." Dad continues, "Rachel went shopping at a store named Bruno's, and she bought a large pillow. All of her old pillows were eaten by a creature living in her house. That creature is a . . ." Keith continues, "Dinosaur! There is a dinosaur living at Rachel's house and sleeping in her bed and eating her pillows." Dad adds, "The dinosaur's name is Crunchy and he is blue. His name is Crunchy because he eats all of Rachel's food and furniture. Some of the things he likes to eat are . . ." Keith says, "Pillows, chairs, tables, TVs, ice cream, and chocolate chip cookies. Crunchy also likes to drink chocolate milk." Dad continues, "Rachel is planning to bring Crunchy on vacation soon. They are planning to go to . . ." Keith ends with, "the beach, because Crunchy wants to go swimming in the ocean."

HINTS AND VARIATIONS

- 💡 To keep the story alive, adults may end their story segments with a leading sentence, as shown in the example.
- 💡 To continue the story after you get home, ask your preschooler to draw a picture of the main character.
- 💡 Pointing out visual clues about the stranger is a good way to generate ideas for continuing the story.
- 💡 In the next round, have players link the new character to the previous one. The new character can be related to or acquainted with the previous character, and other characters can be built into the story in some capacity.
- 💡 After you have played this game a few times, encourage your child to increase the length of his turn each time; that is, add more than one or two sentences.

SKILLS DEVELOPED: This fairly unstructured game is a great way to encourage your preschool child to think creatively. Basing the stories on strangers sparks young imaginations. Storytelling is also great practice for using language and communicating thoughts and ideas. Encourage your child to speak in complete sentences, and introduce new vocabulary words to him through the stories.

SALT AND PEPPER

PURPOSE: To sharpen visual observation, counting, and verbal response skills.

MATERIALS NEEDED: None

NUMBER OF PLAYERS: 2 or more

HOW TO PLAY: One player is designated Salt and the other Pepper. Salt looks for white cars and Pepper looks for black cars. Every time Salt spots a white car, he calls out "Salt!" Every time Pepper spots a black car, she calls out "Pepper!"

EXAMPLE: Owen is Salt and Lily is Pepper. Owen spots two white cars and says "Salt! Salt!" Lilly spots one black car and says "Pepper!" They play until they reach their destination.

HINTS AND VARIATIONS

- Assign the Salt and Pepper roles by having a race to spot the first white car. The first person to call out "Salt!" is designated Salt for the game and the other player is designated Pepper.
- With three players, call this the Patriotic Game and assign Red, White, and Blue to each player. Red says "Red!" when she sees a red car, and so forth.
- With four players, assign two Salts and two Peppers.
- Points may be awarded for each Salt car and for each Pepper car that is spotted.
- Continue the game on your next car ride. If points are awarded and scores are tracked, the person with the lowest score can select whether he'll be Salt or Pepper on the next car ride. Players start counting from where they left off on the last trip.
- For variation, switch to types of automobiles rather than colors. Minivans, trucks, and station wagons may be assigned instead of colors.
- Instead of cars, focus on street signs. One player can be assigned the green signs, one player the red, and one player the yellow. Award bonus points when players identify the words on the signs.

SKILLS DEVELOPED: Because playing *Salt and Pepper* requires participants to focus their attention outside their own cars, it's a great way to relieve boredom during any car trip. By searching for cars of certain colors, children are strengthening their observation skills. When players strive to respond quickly by calling out "Salt!" or "Pepper!," they are practicing their verbal skills. Keeping track of how many cars of each color have been spotted requires concentration; while the counting activity promotes problem-solving skills.

ALPHABET ONE, TWO, THREE

PURPOSE: To sharpen visual observation, letter-recognition, counting, and verbal response skills.

MATERIALS NEEDED: None

NUMBER OF PLAYERS: 2 or more

HOW TO PLAY: In the first round, the youngest player picks a letter. Everyone looks outside the car for objects or words (printed on signs, stores, trucks, and so on) that begin with that letter. When a player spots an object or word, she calls it out. Each player keeps track of how many objects or words he has spotted, and the round continues until one player has found and called out three. That player selects another letter for the next round.

EXAMPLE: Delaney selects the first letter. She chooses D. Alex spots a dog and calls it out (his first D word). Mom calls out a billboard for DeLuca's (her first D word) and a Dodge Caravan (her second D word). Delaney sees another dog and calls it out (her first D word), and Alex spots and calls out a train depot (his second D word) and a driveway (his third D word). Alex has identified and called out three D words, so he starts the next round by selecting the letter S. The family continues playing until they reach their destination.

HINTS AND VARIATIONS

- Don't move on to the next round until every player has located at least one object or word that begins with the selected letter.

- In a simpler version of this game (also a variation for playing after dark), players *think* of words that begin with the designated letter rather than *look* for objects or words. Players track the number of words named until one player reaches three.

- In another variation, players simply look for objects or words that begin with the designated letter, but do not keep track of how many words have been named. This is a good way to introduce the game to preschoolers. Once the game has been mastered, you can move on to the traditional version where scores are tracked.

- In a noncompetitive version, instead of having the first player to reach three pick the next letter, simply take turns doing this.

SKILLS DEVELOPED: Like the *Salt and Pepper* game, *Alphabet One, Two, Three* requires participants to focus their attention outside the car, making it a fun way to pass the time on a long road trip or a routine trip. However, finding objects and words that begin with a particular letter is more challenging than finding colors. As players search, they are strengthening both their observation skills and their problem-solving skills. Some preschoolers think out loud and verbalize many of the objects they see until they find the word that begins with the right sound.

Alphabet One, Two, Three reinforces alphabet sounds. You may want to delay the counting part of this game until children have mastered the phonetic component. Once players are ready to count, they are further exercising their problem-solving skills and concentration abilities.

OPPOSITES

PURPOSE: To sharpen listening, problem-solving, and language skills by finding antonyms.

MATERIALS NEEDED: None

NUMBER OF PLAYERS: 2 or more

HOW TO PLAY: With two players, the adult says a word and the pre-schooler responds with its opposite. (See Hints and Variations for suggested starting words.) With more than two players, the adult says a word and the children take turns calling out its opposite.

EXAMPLE: Dad, Jill, and Anne are riding in the car. Dad says "hot" and Jill responds with "cold." Then Dad says "hello" and Anne answers "good-bye." Dad says "dull" and Jill responds with "shiny." Dad says "short" and Anne says "tall." The game continues until they reach their destination.

HINTS AND VARIATIONS

- Examples of opposite pairs include: Beginning, end. Start, finish. Clean, dirty. Big, little. High, low. Beautiful, ugly. Day, night. Light, dark. Black, white. Soft, hard. Easy, hard. Right, left. Nice, mean. Flat, round. Young, old. Old, new. Front, back. Neat, messy. Early, late. Warm, cool. Loud, soft. Hungry, full. Stop, go. Save, spend. Straight, crooked. Fast, slow. Top, bottom. Open, closed. On, off. Many, few. Before, after. Up, down. Polite, rude. Above, below. Empty, full. Borrow, return. Tomorrow, yesterday. Under, over. In, out. Inside, outside. Freeze, melt. Good, bad. Wet, dry. Asleep, awake. Bright, dim. Happy, sad. All, none. Everybody, nobody. Wide, narrow.

☼ If you are playing with more than one child and the players are evenly matched, you may make this game more competitive by asking them to call out each opposite as quickly as they can.

SKILLS DEVELOPED: The first skill is auditory observation. Players must listen to the starting word, then use their problem-solving skills to determine its opposite, and then respond verbally. Playing *Opposites* will help expand your child's vocabulary. Once your child has mastered this game, a natural next step is the following *Rhymin' Simon* game, which is similar in structure but considerably more challenging.

RHYMIN' SIMON

PURPOSE: To sharpen listening, problem-solving, and language skills by finding words that rhyme.

MATERIALS NEEDED: None

NUMBER OF PLAYERS: 2 or more

HOW TO PLAY: In the first round, an adult or other older player selects a starting word that has several words that rhyme with it (refer to Hints and Variations for suggestions). Players take turns naming words that rhyme with the starting word. If a player can't think of a word, she may skip her turn. The round ends when no players can think of another rhyming word. The last player to think of a word selects a new word for the next round, with suggestions from an adult if necessary.

EXAMPLE: Mom selects the word *bat*. The following dialogue occurs between Mom, Elizabeth, Audrey, and Tess.

Elizabeth:	Hat.
Audrey:	Sat.
Tess:	Mat.
Mom:	Gnat.
Tess:	What's a gnat?
Mom:	A small bug.
Elizabeth:	I can't think of a word. I'll skip my turn.
Audrey:	Cat.
Tess:	Fat.
Mom:	Vat.
Elizabeth:	Splat.
Audrey:	I don't know.
Tess:	At.
Mom:	Pat.
Elizabeth:	Tat.
Audrey:	What's a tat?
Elizabeth:	Like in "tit for tat."
Audrey:	Flat.
Tess:	I can't think of anything.
Mom:	Me neither.
Elizabeth:	Me neither.
Audrey:	I said the last word, so pick the first word for the next round.
Mom:	Audrey, how about starting off the next round with either "kite" or "fry?"
Audrey:	OK, how about "fry."

HINTS AND VARIATIONS

- Other good B starting words are: back, bad, bag, ball, bass, bay, bear, bed, bell, bet, bid, bike, bill, bird, bit, bite, blow, bob, bog, boo, bore, boss, bow, boy, bun, bye.

- To introduce this game to children for the first time, it may be run in a less-structured format where players can call out rhyming words as they think of them, rather than waiting their turn. Playing in this free-for-all format for several rounds helps familiarize children with the game and practice generating ideas.

- Older players should feel free to name rhyming words that won't be familiar to everyone. It's an opportunity to introduce new words and explain their meaning to younger players.

- When younger players are stumped, older players may coach them by walking through the alphabet and trying different letters in front of the starting word.

- In a less competitive version, rotate the assignment of selecting the next word rather than awarding this responsibility to the last player who identified a rhyming word.

- The larger a player's vocabulary, the more proficient he is likely to be at playing *Rhymin' Simon*. Preschool children with limited vocabularies may become frustrated at first. Adults and older children will find it easier, so it's important to de-emphasize the competition in this game, play it with a spirit of cooperation and helpfulness, and use it to build your preschool child's vocabulary.

- Start a rhyme list when you get home. You or your child can write down the rhyming words named in the game you just played.

SKILLS DEVELOPED: The first skill is auditory observation. Listening carefully to the starting word is critical, as well as to the words called out by all the players. Younger players may make the common mistake of calling out words that sound similar to the starting word but are not rhymes, such as *clam* and *man*. Encourage children to evaluate each response and judge whether it's a true rhyme or not. This further develops auditory observation skills.

Problem-solving skills are also developed. It is interesting to observe how children go about generating a rhyming word. Do they seem to think of rhyming words spontaneously, or do they mentally sequence through the alphabet, trying out different starting sounds?

LICENSE PLATE COUNTING

PURPOSE: To sharpen visual observation and problem-solving skills by using license plate numbers to count from 1 to 9.

MATERIALS NEEDED: None

NUMBER OF PLAYERS: 2 or more

HOW TO PLAY: The object is to work together as a team to count from one to nine by spotting these digits on license plates. Players take turns finding the next number. The first player searches for a one. Once he has found it, the next player looks for a two and so on, until all digits have been found in order. Several rounds may be played.

EXAMPLE: Lucia is the first to spot a one on a license plate, so she calls out "One." Mario spots a two and says "Two." Then Dad sees a three and calls it out. It is Lucia's turn again, and she spies and calls out a four. Play continues in this rotating fashion (Lucia, Mario, Dad) until all the digits are spotted. Then they play another round.

HINTS AND VARIATIONS

- A more advanced version of this game is to find all the numbers in the family phone number (in sequence).
- Instead of looking for numbers on license plates, players may look for numbers on signs, in house numbers, or in any other location.
- If there are four or more players, create two teams and have them race against each other to spot all the digits in order.

SKILLS DEVELOPED: Searching exercises observation skills, while figuring out which number is next exercises problem-solving skills.

LICENSE PLATE NAME GAME

PURPOSE: To sharpen visual observation and problem-solving skills by searching for letters to spell out names.

MATERIALS NEEDED: None

NUMBER OF PLAYERS: 2 or more

HOW TO PLAY: Players select the name of a person in the car, then work together to spell out that name by searching for each letter on license plates. Players call out the letters in the correct order as the letters are spotted. The player who spots the last letter has her name spelled in the next round. If her name has already been spelled in a previous round, she may choose another player's name.

EXAMPLE: Samantha, Quinn, Mom, and Jacki decide to spell Jacki's name first. Everyone searches license plates of passing cars to spot the first letter. Quinn sees it first, calling out "J!" Mom asks Jacki to announce the second letter in her name, and everyone then looks for the letter A. Samantha calls it out when she spots it. Jacki announces that C is the next letter, then sees a C herself and calls it out. Samantha finds the next letter, K. Quinn finishes by finding an I. Quinn's name is spelled next. He starts the next round by telling everyone to look for the letter Q.

HINTS AND VARIATIONS

- ☼ Until children know how to spell each family member's name, it may be necessary for an adult to prompt the next letter, as in the example above.
- ☼ One variation is to rotate the letter search around the car, rather than having everyone call out letters as he spots them. One player

would be responsible for spotting the first letter, the next would be responsible for spotting the second letter, and so on until the word is spelled.

-☆- In a competitive version, the players race against each other to spell their own name first. All players try to spell their names out loud simultaneously. This variation can be confusing unless participants have already mastered the basic game.

-☆- Once all the players' names have been spelled, then names of other people, names of animals, or other words can be spelled.

-☆- Advanced players may create a word chain. A starting word or name is selected, but the next word selected must begin with the last letter of the first word. Once that word has been spelled, the next word selected must begin with the last letter of the previous word. The player who found the last letter in the previous word may choose the next word in the chain.

-☆- Rather than looking for letters on license plates, look for letters on street signs, trucks, buildings, or any other location (other than license plates).

SKILLS DEVELOPED: Like other car games, the *License Plate Name Game* requires participants to focus their attention outside the car and concentrate on the world around them. Searching stimulates the observation skills of the players, but the more challenging task is determining which letter is next and creating a word chain (if that variation is used). These activities exercise the problem-solving skills of preschoolers.

ANALOGIES

PURPOSE: To generate and explain analogies using logic and imagination.

MATERIALS NEEDED: None

NUMBER OF PLAYERS: 2 or more

HOW TO PLAY: The youngest person selects a type of food. All the players think of a nonfood object that the food reminds them of and why. Each player recites the following sentence and fills in the blanks: "[Food] is like a [nonfood] because [reason]. Rotate around the car, and give each player a chance to select the starting food.

EXAMPLE: Jay is the youngest in the car. He selects pepperoni as the starting food. Claire says, "Pepperoni is like a Frisbee because it is flat and round." Jay adds, "Pepperoni is like a red plate because it is red and flat and round." Mom states, "Pepperoni is like a tree that is chopped down and then cut into slices, because it is shaped like a long, thin tube at first, and then it is cut into flat, round slices." Now it is Claire's turn to choose the starting food. She selects broccoli. Jay says, "Broccoli is like a tree because it is green and has the same shape as a tree." Claire notes, "Broccoli is like an umbrella because it is narrow at the bottom and wide at the top." Play continues for a few more rounds.

HINTS AND VARIATIONS

- ※ This is a challenging game, and preschool children may be able to play only one or two rounds the first time it is introduced.
- ※ It can be difficult for young children to understand the concept of analogies. Lead by example rather than correcting their selections.

- 🔅 Adults should take their turn last, after the more obvious analogies have been identified by younger children.
- 🔅 In a competitive version, award a point for each analogy identified.
- 🔅 Change the category for the starting words from food to another subject area, such as nature. For example, a flower is like fireworks, a leaf is like a boat, a tree is like a pencil, an acorn is like a cup, a pinecone is like a house, grass is like hair, dirt is like sugar.

SKILLS DEVELOPED: *Analogies* gives your preschooler the opportunity to be highly creative and use his imagination to generate analogies that make sense. This demanding game also encourages your child to express himself clearly as he explains and justifies his selection.

THESAURUS

PURPOSE: To sharpen problem-solving skills, strengthen auditory observation, and expand vocabulary by generating synonyms.

MATERIALS NEEDED: None

NUMBER OF PLAYERS: 2 or more

HOW TO PLAY: With two players, the adult says a starting word out loud. The child responds by saying a synonym for that word. The adult then says another starting word, and the child responds by saying a synonym for that word. Continue for several rounds.

With three or more players, the adult still says the starting word. The youngest player takes the first turn and responds with a synonym for the starting word. Other players are given the opportunity to think of additional synonyms, one player at a time, in a rotating fashion. In the next round, the adult says another starting word out loud. The next youngest player goes first, responding with a synonym. The other players take turns saying additional synonyms.

EXAMPLE: These are the words Dad, Tristan, and Sierra generated while playing *Thesaurus*:

First Round

Dad:	Chilly.
Tristan:	Cold.
Sierra:	Cool.

Second Round

Dad:	Bright.
Sierra:	Colorful.
Tristan:	Sunny.

Third Round

Dad:	Seat.
Tristan:	Chair.
Sierra:	Couch.

Fourth Round

Dad:	Sprinkling.
Sierra:	Raining.
Tristan:	I can't think of another word.
Sierra:	I know one! How about pouring?

Fifth Round

Dad:	Home.
Tristan:	House.
Sierra:	Castle.

Play continues for several more rounds.

HINTS AND VARIATIONS

- It is best for adults to generate the starting words, at least until players are quite proficient at this game.
- The starting word should be the least common word. For example, instead of *raining,* lead with *sprinkling.* Preschoolers are more likely to respond with *raining,* the more common word.
- This game can be played at a slow pace. Give players plenty of time to think of synonyms.
- To make this game more competitive, you may keep score. Award one point to the player who says the first synonym, two points to the player who says the second synonym for the same word, three points to the player who says the third synonym, and so on.
- Don't be literal. It's acceptable for the synonyms to have slightly different meanings than the starting word. This can be a good opportunity to discuss the similarities and differences among the meanings.
- Ask players to use each synonym in a different sentence.
- Use this game as an opportunity to introduce new vocabulary words.

SKILLS DEVELOPED: Playing *Thesaurus* is enjoyable for preschoolers and somewhat challenging for the adult who must generate the starting words. This game strengthens both problem-solving and language abilities. It will also add a new dimension to your preschooler's vocabulary by familiarizing her with different words that have similar meanings. Discussing the distinctions and nuances among the words will help preschool children refine their comprehension and recall abilities (for example, sprinkling, raining, pouring, and precipitation each have different meanings). Use the words in different sentences to demonstrate the shades of differences.

IMAGINARY PIZZA

PURPOSE: To use auditory observation, memory, creativity, and language to create and recall imaginary pizzas.

MATERIALS NEEDED: None

NUMBER OF PLAYERS: 2 or more

HOW TO PLAY: The first player begins by saying, "I'm going to top my imaginary pizza with cheese." The next player repeats the sentence and adds another topping to the pizza. The next player repeats the sentence and adds a third topping. Play continues until one player cannot recall all the previous ingredients. Then a new round is started by the last player to name all the pizza toppings in the previous round.

EXAMPLE: This is how Mom, Kate, and Beth topped their imaginary pizza:

> *Kate:*   I'm going to top my imaginary pizza with cheese.
>
> *Beth:*   I'm going to top my imaginary pizza with cheese and broccoli.
>
> *Mom:*   I'm going to top my imaginary pizza with cheese and broccoli and chocolate chips.
>
> *Kate:*   I'm going to top my imaginary pizza with cheese and broccoli and chocolate chips and orange slices.
>
> *Beth:*   I'm going to top my imaginary pizza with cheese and chocolate chips and orange slices and jelly.

Kate points out that Beth had missed a topping. Beth couldn't recall the missing topping, so the round ended. Kate was the last person to remember the full list, so she went first in the next round.

HINTS AND VARIATIONS

- ☀ Cheese should be the first topping in every round, but none of the other toppings should be repeated in subsequent rounds on the same road trip. For example, if the toppings in the first round are cheese, broccoli, and chocolate chips, then broccoli and chocolate chips may not be repeated in subsequent rounds.
- ☀ As the game progresses, add even more outrageous toppings. Silly things like eyeballs, caterpillars, and crayons will make the game more fun.
- ☀ This can be a challenging game for young preschool children. An easier version is for each player to repeat the one ingredient added on the previous turn, rather than repeating all the previous ingredients. Once this version has been mastered, then increase the difficulty slightly by moving up to repeating the two previous ingredients.
- ☀ When you get home, ask your child to draw a picture of the imaginary pizza that was created.
- ☀ Another variation is called *Expedition*. Rather than build a pizza, players are packing for an expedition. The starting sentence is "I'm going on an expedition and I'm going to bring . . ." Each player adds another item, as in *Imaginary Pizza*.

SKILLS DEVELOPED: Playing *Imaginary Pizza* requires your preschooler to listen carefully and concentrate in order to remember previous ingredients. When it's her turn, an entirely different set of skills is called into play: imagination and communication. She'll use her imagination to think of interesting pizza toppings to add, and her communication skills to convey these toppings to the other players with flair and humor.

WORD CHAINS

PURPOSE: To identify beginning and ending sounds in words, sharpen problem-solving skills, and expand vocabulary.

MATERIALS NEEDED: None

NUMBER OF PLAYERS: 2 or more

HOW TO PLAY: The first player begins by saying a word out loud. The second player must call out another word that begins with the same letter that the previous word ended with. The third player calls out another word in the same manner. The word chain grows as play continues. Words may not be repeated. When a player gets stumped, the round ends. The last player to add a word to the word chain starts the next round with a new word.

EXAMPLE: Mom, Dad, Sarah, Jacob, and Adam created the following word chain:.

Jacob:	Elephant.
Adam:	Tree.
Dad:	Egg.
Sarah:	Gopher.
Mom:	Rainbow.
Jacob:	Wasp.
Adam:	Penny.
Dad:	Yell.
Sarah:	Lion.
Mom:	Nest.
Jacob:	Truck.
Adam:	Kangaroo.

Dad:	Orange.
Sarah:	Eat.
Mom:	Twin.

Play continues until one player is stumped. Then the previous player starts the next round with a new word.

HINTS AND VARIATIONS

- For young players, have them first say the last letter of the previous word. Ask them to guess again if they name an incorrect letter. After the correct letter has been established, give them time to think of a word beginning with that letter.
- Play this game at a relaxed pace and give young players plenty of time to think of the next word in the chain.
- A more advanced version requires all the words in the word chain to have something in common. For example, they can be types of animals, food, or toys. Older children can play this game with the names of locations (cities, towns, states, countries, and so forth).
- Use this game as an opportunity to introduce new vocabulary words.

SKILLS DEVELOPED: The primary skill is letter sound recognition. Players learn to listen carefully to identify letter sounds. They must also use problem-solving skills to generate words that begin with the appropriate letters. This word recall component of the game is good practice for using word recall in everyday communication. When new words are introduced during the game, it also becomes a way of building vocabularies.

Word Chains requires concentration, and an adult can help keep the group focused by facilitating and asking questions.

LACE RACE

PURPOSE: To exercise fine motor skills and counting skills by lacing yarn through numbered holes.

MATERIALS NEEDED: Cardboard or poster board, hole punch, marker or pen, yarn, tape

NUMBER OF PLAYERS: 1 or more

HOW TO PLAY: Before the car trip, create simple lacing boards. Cut a basic shape such as a star or a house out of a piece of cardboard or poster board. Punch several holes in the shape. Number the holes on one side, then turn the shape over and number the holes on the other side in a different sequence. Cut a long piece of yarn and tape one end of the yarn to the center of the lacing board.

During the car ride, give each player a lacing board. They must thread the yarn in and out of the holes, following the sequence according to the numbers. When they've finished, have them pull out the yarn, turn the lacing board over, and use the numbers on the other side to relace the holes in the board in a new sequence.

EXAMPLE: Mom creates four lacing boards for Brian, Kevin, Colleen, and Maureen in the shapes of a star, moon, sun, and cloud. Each shape has twenty holes, a set of numbers written on each side, and a piece of yarn taped to its center.

On the road trip, Mom hands out the lacing boards to the children. Each child laces her board and then shows them to the other kids. Then they remove the yarn from the holes, flip the boards over, and relace them. Mom suggests a lace race. Because Kevin is the youngest, he is allowed to start first. The other three children join in, racing to thread their laces through all twenty holes in order. Once the race is completed, each child passes his board to the player on the left, giving each other the opportunity to try lacing a new shape.

HINTS AND VARIATIONS

- 💡 There are many options for materials. For the board itself, you may recycle old manila folders, notebook covers, or the cardboard backs of notepads. The material must be stiff enough for threading, yet not so heavy that it will be difficult to punch holes.
- 💡 Wrap a piece of tape around the end of the yarn to make it easier to thread. You may substitute string or colorful ribbon for the yarn.
- 💡 For more intricate shapes, trace large cookie cutters.
- 💡 After the road trip, the children may decorate their lacing boards at home using markers, glitter, glue, stickers, paint, or other art materials.

SKILLS DEVELOPED: This activity/game focuses on two major skills: counting and dexterity. It requires manual dexterity to thread the yarn in and out of the holes, and the numbers reinforce counting and sequencing skills. Decorating the boards when you get home is a great way to extend the game beyond the car and stimulate artistic expression.

SPONTANEOUS

PURPOSE: To challenge a child's imagination as well as his problem-solving, listening, and language skills.

MATERIALS NEEDED: None

NUMBER OF PLAYERS: 2 or more

HOW TO PLAY: The first player begins by saying any word out loud. The second player responds by saying a word that is related to that word. The third player says a word related to the word that the second player said. Play continues, with each player adding a word.

EXAMPLE: Alex says the first word, "Honey." Michaela says "Bee." Mom says "Sting." Dad says "Pain." Alex: "Cry." Michaela: "Laugh." Mom: "Party." Dad: "Games." Alex: "Soccer." Michaela: "Ball." Mom: "Round." Dad: "Square." Alex: "Box." Michaela: "Present." Mom: "Wrap." Dad: "Ribbon." The game continues for several minutes.

HINTS AND VARIATIONS

- Remind players to base their response on the immediate previous word, not the word that was called out two or three turns ago. This is the only guideline; otherwise, there are no right or wrong answers to this game.
- You may need to define a word before a child is able to respond. Use this game as an opportunity to introduce new vocabulary words.
- You may play this game by using categories such as animals, people, characters, foods, books, or toys.

SKILLS DEVELOPED: *Spontaneous* is a free-flowing and creative game for children of all ages. It primarily relies on auditory observation skills, as the players listen to and process words called out on previous turns. Players use their imagination and language skills to select their own word. They also use problem-solving skills to determine whether the word they have selected is related to the immediate previous word and not a word from two or three turns ago. Play this game at a relaxed pace and discuss the group's answers and new vocabulary words.

LIST MAKER

PURPOSE: To use imagination, language, and artistic expression to create pictorial lists, and to use problem-solving skills and visual observation to check off items on the list.

MATERIALS NEEDED: Paper; crayons, markers, or pencils; stickers (optional)

NUMBER OF PLAYERS: 1 or more

HOW TO PLAY: Before a long car trip, have your preschoolers each make a list of objects they think they will see from the car window. The items on each list may be illustrated with hand-drawn pictures, computer clip art, stickers, or words. Ask the children to draw a small box next to each picture. On the road trip, each child brings his list as well as a pencil or crayon. As the child spots items on the list, he calls them out and checks them off.

EXAMPLE: Before their car trip, Mason and Eve create lists. Eve's list is made up of stickers and drawings, and next to each item she draws a small box. Her list includes a tricycle, truck, large building, bird, dog, lady, man, flower, cat, and squirrel. Mason's list is written using words that Mom helped him spell. His words include fence, McDonald's, stop sign, wheelbarrow, fire truck, cactus, mail truck, minivan, boat, and gas station. He draws a small box next to each word. On the car trip, Eve and Mason look out the window to find the items on their list. As each item is spotted, Mason and Eve call it out and then put a check mark or an X in the box next to that item.

HINTS AND VARIATIONS

- Players should have at least ten items on each list. Some of these items should be something that isn't commonly found.

-🔆- Children who are learning to read and write may create a list using words that are spelled with help from an adult.

-🔆- Adults can write words to label the pictures on the list.

-🔆- Children may need a lesson on how to draw a check mark. Instead of using a check mark, players may write an X in the box or color in the box with a crayon.

-🔆- To make this game competitive, an adult assigns points to each item on the list. Easy items are worth one point, medium items are worth two points, and difficult items are worth three points. Players race to earn a certain number of points, such as fifteen, or players count the number of points they've earned by the end of the road trip. Adults and children may also work together to decide how points are to be assigned.

-🔆- If you're driving to a vacation destination, the list may be expanded to cover things that children expect to see during the vacation, not just from the car.

SKILLS DEVELOPED: Kids enjoy creating lists and checking things off, so *List Maker* can make a long car ride more enjoyable. In the preparation stage, children use their imagination to select items to include on their list, and they use artistic skills to draw pictures to illustrate the list. Older players may use language and expression to write words that appear on the list.

Even if your child's drawings are not representational and cannot be deciphered by others, chances are she will remember what the drawing is meant to depict. It's a good idea for an adult to label the drawings with words for two reasons: First, seeing labels next to drawings encourages letter recognition and prereading skills. Second, if the child forgets what a drawing is meant to depict, an adult can refer to the written word.

Once the car ride begins, children use their visual observation skills to search for the items on their lists and their problem-solving skills to compare what they see to what is on the list. Checking items off the list using small check marks or X's exercises fine motor skills and gives players a sense of accomplishment.

APPLES FOR MY TEACHER

PURPOSE: To develop simple math skills using problem-solving skills and auditory observation.

MATERIALS NEEDED: None

NUMBER OF PLAYERS: 2 or more

HOW TO PLAY: The first player selects a number from one to five to indicate the number of apples she will give to her teacher. The next player tells everyone how many apples he will give to the teacher (also a number between one and five), and how many apples the teacher will now have in total. The next player does the same, with each player giving a few more apples to the teacher (or taking a few apples away) and stating the current sum. Keep playing until the teacher has more than fifteen or twenty apples.

EXAMPLE: Sarah, Emily, and Mom shared the following dialogue:

Sarah:	I'll give my teacher two apples.
Emily:	I'll give her two more, so now she'll have four.
Mom:	I'll give her one more. Now she'll have five, because four plus one equals five.
Sarah:	I'll give her two more. Two plus five equals seven, so now she'll have seven apples.
Emily:	I'll give her one more. Seven plus one equals eight. Now she'll have eight apples.

| Mom: | The teacher has eight apples, and I'll take away one. Eight minus one is seven. Now she'll have seven apples. |
| Sarah: | The teacher has seven apples, and I'll give her three more. Now she'll have nine. |

That is an incorrect answer, so it's time to start a new round. Mom was the last player to give a correct answer, so she begins the new round.

Mom:	I'll give the teacher four apples.
Sarah:	The teacher has four apples, and I'll give her one more. Four plus one equals five, so now the teacher has five apples.
Emily:	The teacher has five apples, and I'll take away three. Five minus three equals two. Now she has two apples.

The game continues until a player calls out an incorrect sum, and then a new round is started.

HINTS AND VARIATIONS

- Give preschool children a second chance to determine the correct sum if their initial answer is incorrect.
- As a group, count the number of turns taken in a round to encourage the math problem to continue.
- Introduce subtraction when children can understand it.
- The adult should act as a "controller," adding or subtracting apples to keep the numbers within a reasonable range.
- Older children may be able to handle larger numbers, so the number of apples added may be between one and ten. Also, you may raise the end point from twenty apples to forty or higher.
- A simple variation is simply to call out math problems to calculate, such as "What's three plus four?" Once preschoolers have

mastered simple addition problems, they may be ready to progress to the traditional version of this game.

- ☀ If kids aren't ready to perform calculations in their head, this game may be played at home using pennies or other small items. In the car, players may use their fingers to count. In this variation, set ten as the maximum number of apples that the teacher can receive.

SKILLS DEVELOPED: Doing math problems can be particularly satisfying for children. Playing *Apples for My Teacher* takes simple addition problems to the next level. Children must use their auditory observation skills to listen to and process what the other players say, then use their mathematical problem-solving skills to calculate the sum. Repeating the same words each turn minimizes confusion.

CRAZY EIGHTS

PURPOSE: To develop the understanding of subtraction using problem-solving skills and auditory observation.

MATERIALS NEEDED: None

NUMBER OF PLAYERS: 2 or more

HOW TO PLAY: An adult selects a number from one to eight and incorporates it into this sentence: "I have four pennies, but I wish I had eight." The first player states how many pennies must be added to the adult's pile in order for the adult to have eight pennies. Then the adult selects a new number from one to eight and says it aloud in the same sentence for the next player. The next player states how many pennies must be added to the pile in order for the adult to have eight pennies. Continue playing for several rounds.

EXAMPLE

Dad:	I have four pennies, but I wish I had eight. Ali, how many pennies do I need to get eight?
Ali:	Four.
Dad:	That's right. Four plus four is eight. But now I have five pennies, but I wish I had eight. Amy, how many pennies do I need to get eight?
Amy:	Three.
Dad:	That's right. Five plus three is eight. Now I have six pennies, but I wish I had eight. Ali, How many pennies do I need to get eight?
Ali:	Three.
Dad:	Guess again.
Ali:	Two.

The game continues for several rounds.

HINTS AND VARIATIONS

- Give children a second chance to determine the correct sum if their initial answer is incorrect.
- After each correct answer, restate the question in the form of an addition problem, such as "Three plus five is eight."
- Once you've covered all the possible combinations of eight a few times, play *Crazy Sevens* or *Crazy Nines*.
- In a variation, start with numbers larger than eight, and ask players how many numbers must be taken away from the pile in order to create eight.
- If preschoolers are just beginning to understand the concept of subtraction, this game may be simplified by calling out easy subtraction problems, such as "What's eight minus four?"

- 🔆 Once this game has been mastered, give the children a chance to lead by stating the math problems.
- 🔆 If kids aren't ready to perform calculations in their head, play at home using pennies or other small items.

SKILLS DEVELOPED: The leap from understanding addition to understanding subtraction is a big one, and this game makes that leap more fun. Preschoolers must use their auditory observation skills to listen to and process the math problem posed by the adult. When it's their turn to respond, they use their mathematical problem-solving skills to calculate the answer. Play this game at a slow pace and provide abundant support and encouragement, because early efforts can be frustrating.

HI, MY NAME IS ALICE

PURPOSE: To use imagination, problem-solving skills, auditory observation, and language to create a description of a person, with all the key words beginning with the same letter.

MATERIALS NEEDED: None

NUMBER OF PLAYERS: 2 or more

HOW TO PLAY: Play rotates around the car, with the first player creating a description based on the letter A, the second player based on the letter B, the third player C, and so on. On his turn, each player completes the following sentence: "Hi, my name is _____ and my brother's (or sister's) name is _____. We come from _____ and we sell _____." Female players create a brother's name and male players create a sister's name.

EXAMPLE

> *A:*   Hi, my name is Alice and my brother's name is Al. We come from Alabama and we sell apples.
>
> *B:*   Hi, my name is Brett, my sister's name is Brianna. We come from Boston and we sell boxes.
>
> *C:*   Hi, my name is Charlie and my sister's name is Chelsea. We come from California and we sell candles.
>
> *D:*   Hi, my name is Donald and my sister's name is Delila. We come from DisneyWorld and we sell ducks.

The game continues until the players complete a description for each letter of the alphabet.

HINTS AND VARIATIONS

- Take your time with this game. It may take children a while to develop a complete description for a person.

- When a child is stumped on a word, offer him a multiple-choice clue. For example, if a child can't think of a place beginning with the letter D, give him a few choices, such as DisneyWorld, Boston, and California, and let him select the word that begins with D.

- The most challenging word in the description will be the place. Introduce new places that your children may not be familiar with, and explain where they are and what they're like. When you get home, show children where the places are on a map or globe.

- The places don't need to be specific. You can use such descriptions as an apple orchard or a dinosaur den.

- Players may choose their own alphabet letter rather than starting with A.

- Silly names, places, and items make this game more fun.

- When children are ready for more complexity, add a food item to the end of the last sentence: ". . . and we eat _____." Players must name a food that begins with the appropriate letter to complete this sentence.

☀ When you get home, ask the children to draw a picture of one of the "people" they described.

SKILLS DEVELOPED: Children love using their imagination to create made-up people with strange names from faraway places. They use problem-solving skills to find words that begin with the appropriate letter, and this activity helps build prereading skills. Continuing the game when you get home by referring to a map or drawing a picture enhances the overall experience, adding significance to the people created.

ROADSIDE CRIBBAGE

PURPOSE: To use visual observation skills by searching for particular objects, and to use problem-solving skills to add up points and distinguish right from left.

MATERIALS NEEDED: None

NUMBER OF PLAYERS: 2 or more

HOW TO PLAY: Create a Left Team and a Right Team, based on which side of the car players are seated on. Players sitting in the middle may be on either team. Assign point values to objects you expect to see on your road trip. Commonly seen items are worth one point, less commonly seen items are worth two points, and rarely seen items are worth three points. Players look out either the left or the right side of the car, depending on their team. They call out items from the list that they see on their side of the road and tally their points out loud. Cemeteries are "wipeouts," meaning that if a team spots a cemetery on their side, then the other team's points are wiped out to zero. The teams keep score until they reach their destination. The team with most points at the end of the road trip wins.

EXAMPLE: The Right Team is made up of Jenna, Michael, and Mom, and the Left Team is made up of Dad and Alicia. The group establishes point values for six objects they expect to see:

> Cows: 1 point each
> Trailer trucks: 1 point each
> Log piles: 1 point each
> Toll booths: 2 points each
> Gas stations: 2 points each
> Police cars: 3 points each
> Cemeteries: wipeouts

The game begins. Jenna spots a field with four cows on the right side, so the Right Team earns four points. Dad sees a gas station on the left, and the Left Team earns two points. Mom spies a pile of logs on the right, earning the Right Team another point, totaling five. Michael spots a trailer truck on the right, earning another point, so the Right Team has six points. Alicia points out a police car on her side, giving the Left Team three more points, totaling five. Then Alicia sees a cemetery on the left side, so the Right Team's score is wiped out to zero. Jenna spots a pile of logs on the right, earning the Right Team one point. Play continues until they reach their destination. The Right Team earns twenty-nine points and the Left Team earns eighteen points.

HINTS AND VARIATIONS

- ☼ The list should be no longer than four to six objects so that it won't be too confusing or difficult to remember.
- ☼ Begin this game with a review of right versus left for the young players.

- 💡 Ask the children to tally scores.
- 💡 Once you've established a list that seems to work, use it every time you play to make it easier to remember.

SKILLS DEVELOPED: The teamwork and cooperation inherent in this game takes the edge off the competition. As the family works together to come up with the list of objects, imagination, negotiation, and language skills are being practiced. Visual observation skills are sharpened when kids strive to rack up more points than the competing team. Problem-solving skills are exercised when teams tally up the number of points they've accrued.

NAME THAT TUNE

PURPOSE: To guess the titles of familiar songs by using auditory observation and problem solving.

MATERIALS NEEDED: Children's songs on CD or cassette, CD player or tape player

NUMBER OF PLAYERS: 2 or more

HOW TO PLAY: An adult plays the first few seconds of a familiar children's song and then hits the pause button. Players who know the song title are asked to call it out. If no one can name the song title, a few more seconds of the song are played, and players are given the chance to call out the title again. When a player correctly identifies the song title, she earns a point. The adult then plays the first few seconds of another children's song. The game continues for several songs or until the destination is reached.

EXAMPLE: While Mom drives, Dad plays a few seconds of a song from a familiar CD. Neither Monique nor Nicholas can name the tune, so Dad plays a few more seconds of the song. Monique gives a title, but it is incorrect, so Dad plays a few more seconds. Nicholas guesses the correct song title, so he earns one point. Dad begins the next round by playing another song. Monique ultimately guesses the title, so she earns a point. The family continues playing until they reach their destination. Nicholas has accrued seven points and Monique five.

HINTS AND VARIATIONS

- ‑🔅‑ For safety's sake, adults who play the music should be passengers, not drivers.
- ‑🔅‑ Give the players some latitude when naming song titles. They are likely to be imprecise in the names.
- ‑🔅‑ If you're playing a CD that the children are very familiar with, do not play the songs in order; choose songs at random.
- ‑🔅‑ Keeping score is not necessary if you'd like to make the game less competitive.
- ‑🔅‑ Another, less competitive alternative is to give each player his own turn. Play a few seconds of music for one player to guess. If the song title is not guessed correctly, then the next few seconds are played for the next player. Continue rotating around the car, giving each player a turn to guess the song title.

SKILLS DEVELOPED: Listening skills are the key talent stimulated by this game. Language and expression are also challenged, as well as problem-solving skills, as players race to identify and call out the song titles.

NAME THAT SOUND

PURPOSE: To use artistic expression to create a sound-effect tape, and to use listening and problem-solving skills to try to guess the sounds.

MATERIALS NEEDED: Cassette tape, cassette recorder

NUMBER OF PLAYERS: 2 or more

HOW TO PLAY: Before a road trip, one child uses a cassette recorder to record common household and outdoor sounds with the help of an adult. On the road trip, the cassette is played, and the other players guess the source of each sound. One point is awarded for each correct guess.

EXAMPLE: Before a long road trip, Sam and Mom record several sounds on a cassette tape. These sounds include: Dad snoring, running water, the car starting, a video rewinding, the toilet flushing, the bed creaking, the doorbell ringing, the school bus stopping and opening its doors, the mailbox opening, the refrigerator door opening, children playing on the playground, customers ordering lunch at a fast-food restaurant, Julia crying, the computer turning on, the neighbor's dog barking, and a rattle being shaken. During the road trip, Sam and Mom play these sounds. Dad and Julia race each other to guess what is making each sound.

HINTS AND VARIATIONS
- ☀ Sounds must be clear and recognizable. Use a cassette recorder with decent sound quality.
- ☀ Record at least ten sounds. Leave a gap of several seconds between each sound.
- ☀ Make sure that some of the sounds are silly or funny.

- ☀ Start the cassette with a brief message. Introduce the child who is recording the sounds as a world-famous recording artist.
- ☀ Take the tape recorder with you around town one day, recording sounds from different people and places.
- ☀ To make the game more competitive, subtract one point for each incorrect guess.

SKILLS DEVELOPED: Creating the cassette tape allows your child to express herself artistically. Give her the freedom to select the sounds to record, offering suggestions and, of course, vetoing offensive sounds. Show your child how to record the sounds and put a gap between each one, and how to play back the tape to check the quality of the sound. Creating the tape is a challenging but enjoyable task for your child. For the other players, the key skills stimulated by this game are auditory observation skills, as well as problem-solving skills. The whole family is sure to have fun listening to and identifying the sounds on the tape.

SONGWRITER

PURPOSE: To use problem-solving, listening, and language skills to rewrite popular children's songs.

MATERIALS NEEDED: None

NUMBER OF PLAYERS: 2 or more

HOW TO PLAY: An adult identifies a song to be rewritten, such as "Twinkle, Twinkle, Little Star." Players take turns rewriting selected lines from the song.

EXAMPLE: Mom suggests that she and Sophie make up some new lines for the song "Twinkle, Twinkle, Little Star." Mom proposes that they concentrate on rewriting the second line, but that it should still rhyme with the first line. They begin by brainstorming words that rhyme with *star*. Sophie comes up with *far, car, bar, jar,* and *tar*. Based on these ideas, they create the following variations for the second line:

> *Twinkle, twinkle, little star*
> *I can see you from my car.*

> *Twinkle, twinkle, little star*
> *Can I keep you in a jar?*

> *Twinkle, twinkle, little star*
> *As you shine upon the tar.*

> *Twinkle, twinkle, little star*
> *I can't reach you, you're too far.*

Mom then suggests that they focus on rewriting the fourth line to rhyme with "Up above the world so high." Sophie lists several words that rhyme with *high*, including *fry, sigh, cry, die, guy, hi, fly, my, pie, tie,* and *why*. Mom and Sophie create these variations together:

> *Up above the world so high*
> *Like a flying hot french fry.*

> *Up above the world so high*
> *As quiet as a baby's sigh.*

> *Up above the world so high*
> *I can sometimes hear you cry.*

> *Up above the world so high*
> *Shining on each girl and guy.*

Up above the world so high
Winking down and saying hi.

Up above the world so high
Like a flying blueberry pie.

Up above the world so high
Higher than a buzzing fly.

Up above the world so high
Can you see my Daddy's tie?

They select their favorite verses and sing a new version of the song. When they get home, Mom writes it down so they can sing it again on another road trip.

HINTS AND VARIATIONS

- Select a song with words that are easy to rhyme. For ideas, listen to a children's CD or cassette.
- Coach children on which lines of the song you can rewrite together.
- Facilitate the process of identifying the key word in the selected line and generating new rhyming words.
- You may decide that you don't need exact rhymes for the new verses.
- Repeat the new lines a few times to remember them.
- If you have a portable cassette recorder, bring it with you and record the new song when it's complete.

SKILLS DEVELOPED: Generating rhyming words is the basic activity of this game, and this requires problem-solving skills. On the next level, children can participate in generating ideas. Advanced players may even be able to form a complete rhyming line with a good rhythm. Careful listening, taking turns, and respect for others are important success factors in this creative game.

HOME
GAMES

TREASURE HUNT

PURPOSE: To enhance visual observation skills, spatial ability, and imagination through the use of maps.

MATERIALS NEEDED: Paper, pen or pencil, refrigerator magnets, small toy or stuffed animal

NUMBER OF PLAYERS: 2 or more

HOW TO PLAY: Draw a rough map or floor plan of the house (or the location where the game will be played). As you are drawing, explain the map to the players, pointing out the different rooms in the house. When the map is done, have the players turn their backs or close their eyes while you hide a particular toy in one room of the house. Then post the map on the refrigerator using the magnets. Place one magnet on the map as a clue to where the toy is hidden. Using the map, the players try to find the toy. The first player to find the toy hides it in the next round and places the magnet on the map.

EXAMPLE: Dad draws a map of two rooms in the house. He makes rectangles for large pieces of furniture, such as the sofa, the TV, and the bookcase. Brooke and Eli study the map, and then they hide their faces in their hands while Dad hides the teddy bear behind a pillow on the sofa. Dad posts the map on the refrigerator and sticks a magnet on the rectangle that represents the couch. Brooke and Eli follow the map, and eventually Brooke finds the hidden teddy bear. In the next round, Brooke hides the teddy bear and Eli and Dad read the map and hunt for it.

HINTS AND VARIATIONS

- The map can represent one room, a few rooms, or an entire house. This game may also be played outdoors, in which case the map would represent the yard.
- If players are having difficulty finding the hidden toy, the "hider" can give them clues by telling them when they're getting warmer or colder.
- Save the map for playing the game another time.
- Experiment with the degree of difficulty of the hiding places.

SKILLS DEVELOPED: Understanding that a map represents real objects and using the map to find a hidden object helps your child think spatially. Hunting for the hidden toy exercises your child's powers of observation. Thinking of hiding spots for the toy exercises creativity and imagination.

PHOTO CONCENTRATION

PURPOSE: To provide the opportunity for visual observation and artistic expression and the use of memory, problem solving, and motor skills.

MATERIALS NEEDED: Camera, film, 2 sets of developed photos

NUMBER OF PLAYERS: 2 or more

HOW TO PLAY: In the first phase, the players use a camera (with adult supervision) to take photographs of at least six different subjects of their choosing. The film is developed and double prints are obtained.

In the second phase, players select six or more photos to use, along with their duplicates. The photos are shuffled and dealt out facedown on a flat surface. The players take turns turning over two photos at a time to see if they match. If a match is made, the player removes those two photos from the game, places them in her pile, and takes another turn. If they do not match, the player turns the photos facedown again and the next player takes a turn. Play continues until all the photos have been matched and removed from the game.

In the final phase, each player counts the number of photos he collected during the game. You may ask players to compare the totals to see who has collected the most photos, or you may decide not to declare a winner and simply offer congratulations to everyone for playing a fun game.

EXAMPLE: Alex, Maya, and their parents take several photos of their family, friends, and objects inside their home. After two sets of prints are developed, they select eight photos to use in the game. The photos and their duplicates are shuffled and dealt facedown. Alex turns over two photos. They do not match, so he turns them back over, and Maya goes next. The two photos she turns over match. She puts them in her pile and takes another turn. These photos do not match, so she turns them back over, and now it's Mom's turn. The game continues until all the photos have been matched and removed. Then everyone counts the photos in his pile.

HINTS AND VARIATIONS
- When taking photos, encourage the children to take pictures of distinct objects to avoid confusion.
- Use fewer photos to make the game easier, or more photos to make the game more challenging. Increase the number of photos being used as the number of players increases.
- You can skip the first phase by using existing photos.

-✧- You may eliminate the competitive element of this game by not counting the number of photos that each player has at the end of the round.

-✧- If the competitive version of this game is played and players do count the number of photos in their piles at the end of the round, then allow the player with the fewest photos to take the first turn in the next round.

SKILLS DEVELOPED: Taking photos can be a big thrill for preschoolers, and it's a new way for them to express themselves artistically. Reviewing the developed photographs can be a learning experience if it's used as a feedback session on photography. Identify who took each photo and discuss the composition and subject. Selecting the photos can be a fun group activity that enhances communication skills, social skills, and negotiation abilities. Playing the game draws on memory and matching skills. Tallying the photos at the end of the game helps develop counting skills.

M&M SUBTRACTION

PURPOSE: To exercise visual observation skills and counting skills.

MATERIALS NEEDED: M&Ms, cup or mug (nontransparent)

NUMBER OF PLAYERS: 1 or more

HOW TO PLAY: Start with ten M&Ms on a table. Turn the mug upside down and place it next to the M&Ms. Ask the first player to count the M&Ms. Then ask him to close his eyes while you move a few of the candies under the mug. When he opens his eyes, ask him to guess how many M&Ms are under the mug based on the number of M&Ms that are outside the mug. When he guesses correctly, he may eat the candies under the mug.

Have the second player close her eyes. Place one or more of the remaining M&Ms under the mug. Play continues as with the first player. Continue playing until no candies are left. Then start with ten more and play again.

EXAMPLE: Mom places ten M&Ms on the coffee table. Kaitlin counts them and closes her eyes while Mom places two under the mug. When Kaitlin opens her eyes, she counts eight M&Ms remaining. She figures there must be two under the mug. Mom lifts the mug to show that her guess is correct. Kaitlin eats the two M&Ms under the mug.

Next, Christopher closes his eyes while Mom places three of the remaining M&Ms under the mug. When Christopher opens his eyes, he counts five candies outside the mug. He says there are four M&Ms under the mug. Mom asks him to try again. He thinks about it and answers, "Three." Mom lifts the mug to show that he is correct. He eats the three candies.

HINTS AND VARIATIONS

- If you are playing with children of varying ages and abilities, start with a higher number of M&Ms and have the older children guess how many are under the mug in the earlier rounds. As the rounds progress and the numbers get smaller, the game gets easier. Players who are less familiar with the concept of subtraction will be more successful in later rounds.
- Once in a while, don't put any M&Ms under the mug.
- If players are having a difficult time understanding subtraction, show them how to use their fingers or another counting tool to calculate the number of remaining M&Ms.

💡 Raisins, jelly beans, crackers, or any other small food may be substituted for M&Ms.

SKILLS DEVELOPED: This game introduces the concept of subtraction, which can be challenging at first. It works best with children who already understand basic addition. The key skills involved in playing this game are visual observation, as your child must observe the number of M&Ms outside the mug, and counting skills, as your child must count the number of M&Ms inside and outside the mug.

SECRET BOX

PURPOSE: To stimulate your child's imagination and letter-sound-recognition skills.

MATERIALS NEEDED: Empty shoebox (or smaller box) with lid, various household objects

NUMBER OF PLAYERS: 2 or more

HOW TO PLAY: The empty shoebox serves as the Secret Box. One player is designated as Box Keeper. This player selects a household object, discreetly places it inside the Secret Box, and puts the lid over it. The Box Keeper tells the other players the first letter of the object in the Secret Box. The other players take turns guessing what's in the box. The first player to guess correctly becomes the Box Keeper in the next round.

EXAMPLE: Dad is the Box Keeper in the first round. He goes into the kitchen and places a package of Jell-O in the box. He returns to the other players and tells them that the object in the Secret Box begins with the letter J. These are their guesses:

Madeline:	Jump rope?
Jack:	Jelly bean?
Madeline:	A picture of Jack?
Jack:	Jewelry?

Dad gives them a hint. He says the object is a food item.

Madeline:	Juice?
Jack:	Jell-O?

Jack correctly guesses the object, so he becomes Box Keeper for the next round. He goes into the kitchen and places a magnet in the box. He tells Dad and Madeline that the object begins with M. Eventually Madeline guesses magnet, so she becomes Box Keeper. The game continues for several rounds.

HINTS AND VARIATIONS

- An adult should be Box Keeper in the first round.
- Box Keepers who can't give the correct starting letter for the object inside the Secret Box may have an adult assist them.
- Remind children that their guesses must be objects that fit inside the box.
- If players haven't guessed correctly after several tries, the Box Keeper may give a clue.
- After playing for the first time, let the players decorate the Secret Box with glitter glue, stickers, markers, and other art supplies. Each player may want to decorate his or her own Secret Box.

SKILLS DEVELOPED: Children love suspense and surprises. Playing this game is a great way to maintain their interest in generating a list of words that begin with a particular letter. This thinking process stimulates their language and expression skills. Spatial abilities are also called on in this game because children must consider whether their guess is an object that would fit inside the box. Understanding size relationships is a core spatial ability.

COLOR MAKERS

PURPOSE: To create and identify colors using visual observation, problem solving, experimentation, and artistic expression.

MATERIALS NEEDED: Three clear, empty bottles (or clear plastic cups) for each player; several different colors of liquid food coloring; crayons; bowl; paper

NUMBER OF PLAYERS: 1 or more

HOW TO PLAY: Fill the bottles half full with water and give one to each player. Place the crayons in the bowl. Each player closes her eyes and selects a crayon from the bowl. The players open their eyes and use the crayons to draw a scribble or a line on a piece of paper. Have each player pick a food coloring that matches (or closely matches) her crayon color, and add a few drops to the water in her bottle.

Ask the players to predict what will happen if more water is added to their bottles. Compare results with the prediction. Ask the players to select another food coloring to add to their bottles and to predict what color the water will become. Compare results with the prediction. Let each player create a few bottles of colored water.

EXAMPLE: Alyson selects an orange crayon and draws a line on a piece of paper. Because there was no orange food coloring, she chooses yellow. When it is added to the water, the water turns a pale yellow. Alyson's dad suggests adding red. Alyson adds too many drops of red at first, but when she adds more yellow, the color of the water turns orange. Alyson's dad selects a green crayon from the bowl, and he asks Alyson for suggestions for food coloring to add to his water to tint it green.

HINTS AND VARIATIONS

- Instead of crayons, players may use markers or even jelly beans and eat the selected jelly bean when the color has been achieved.
- Ask the players to try to create their favorite color or any color after they've successfully matched a few crayon colors.
- Let the players drop objects into the colored water, such as glitter, pennies, or paper clips. Shake up the bottles.
- Let the players decorate the bottles with permanent markers.
- Pour the colored water in an ice cube tray and freeze it, especially the darker colors. The next day, drop the colored ice cubes into clear glasses filled with room temperature water or Sprite and let the kids predict what color their drink will turn.

SKILLS DEVELOPED: Watching water change colors as food coloring is added is a fascinating activity for preschoolers, and it helps develop their powers of visual observation. Giving children a goal to attain, such as achieving a particular color, adds an element of problem solving. This game also provides an excellent forum for testing and experimentation. Trying to predict which color appears next and asking questions like "What if I add yellow?" are enriching experimentation activities.

When children mix food coloring with water to create their own unique colors, they are given the opportunity to express themselves artistically through the process of color selection and color creation. Creating colored ice cubes and experimenting with them extends the learning and the fun beyond the initial game.

DINNERTIME!

PURPOSE: To exercise your child's listening and problem-solving skills.

MATERIALS NEEDED: Family dinner, play money

NUMBER OF PLAYERS: 2 or more

HOW TO PLAY: Designate one family member as the cashier, and give the other players several dollars of play money. Announce that each family member will have to pay for dinner tonight! Set a price for each food or course in the family meal. As the food is served, the cashier announces the price for each item. As the players eat each food, they must set aside payment for it. At the end of the meal, players add up their total payment and pay the cashier.

EXAMPLE: Each player is given $10 in play money before dinner. As the salad is served, Dad, the cashier, announces that the price is $2. Each player sets aside $2. The other food is brought out, and Dad says the chicken is $3, the squash is $1, and the rice is $1. Each player sets aside $5. When dessert is served, Dad announces that the price is $2. Each player sets aside $2. After dinner, Dad asks the players to pay for their meal. They count the money they had set aside, a total of $9 each, and give it to Dad.

HINTS AND VARIATIONS
- Use coins instead of (or in addition to) dollar bills.
- Offer the players a choice in the foods they may purchase for dinner.
- You may help the players keep their reserve money separate from the money they're setting aside by using envelopes.
- To add a visual observation element, write the price for each food on a nearby chalkboard or message board.
- Give each player a "bill" at the end of dinner.

- 🔆 Instead of playing this game over a real dinner, play food may be used.
- 🔆 An adult or an older child should be the cashier.

SKILLS DEVELOPED: This game makes an everyday activity—eating dinner—more fun. Because players must listen for the prices, they develop listening skills. Counting skills are developed as players designate money for food, and categorization skills are necessary to maintain separate money piles. If an element of choice is factored into this game, decision-making skills are used.

NEWSPAPER NUMBERS

PURPOSE: To teach about sequencing using visual observation and problem-solving and motor skills.

MATERIALS NEEDED: Newspaper; scissors (one pair for each player); paper (one sheet for each player); glue stick or tape (one for each player) (optional)

NUMBER OF PLAYERS: 1 or more

HOW TO PLAY: Give each player a section of newspaper, a pair of scissors, and a piece of paper. The players search through their newspaper for all the numbers from one through ten and cut them out. Assist children with the scissors if necessary. The players then arrange their numbers on the paper in order from lowest to highest, and glue them down if desired.

EXAMPLE: Jonathan cuts out a 7, 5, 2, 4, 1, 3, 6, 8, 10, and 9. He arranges them on the paper in order: 1, 2, 3, 4, 5, 6, 7, 8, 9, and 10.

HINTS AND VARIATIONS

- ☼ Write the numbers one through ten on a blank piece of paper. Make them large enough so players can place their cutouts under these numbers to help them keep track of which numbers they need to find.

- ☼ Instead of a section of the newspaper, give players an advertising circular that has plenty of prices and numbers.

- ☼ Extend the series of numbers depending on how high your child can count. For example, players can cut out numbers from one to twenty.

- ☼ Once your child has mastered putting numbers in ascending order, have players put them in descending order.

- ☼ For a more challenging two-round game, instruct players to cut out any ten numbers from one to twenty, and then arrange them in ascending order, leaving space for the missing numbers. Once everyone is ready to progress to the second round, the players go back to the newspaper to locate and cut out the missing numbers.

- ☼ For older children, set a timer and see how many numbers they can cut out and sequence within a defined period of time.

SKILLS DEVELOPED: Searching for numbers in the newspaper stimulates your child's powers of observation. To sort the numbers in ascending or descending order, your child uses problem-solving skills. This exercise enhances your child's familiarity with numbers and their meaning. Using the scissors and arranging the numbers on the paper improves manual dexterity. This game also demonstrates how newspapers can be used for multiple purposes, and it helps make your child aware of the contents of newspapers.

HOME PHONE

PURPOSE: To exercise sorting and sequencing, as well as memory and fine motor skills.

MATERIALS NEEDED: Seven small index cards, business cards, or slips of paper for each player; pen or pencil

NUMBER OF PLAYERS: 1 or more

HOW TO PLAY: For each player, create a set of seven cards with one digit on each card. Collectively, the set should make up the player's home phone number. Shuffle each player's cards. Each player lays her cards out on a flat surface and then rearranges them until they are in the order of her home phone number.

EXAMPLE: Stacey receives seven cards, with a number written on each one: 1, 2, 2, 5, 8, 8, and 8. She lays them out on a table and rearranges them until they are in the order of her home phone number, 828-1528.

HINTS AND VARIATIONS

- If a player doesn't already have his home phone number memorized, write it down on a separate piece of paper for him to refer to while he's playing the game.
- An easier alternative is to ask players to sort numbers from one to ten in ascending order.
- Once players have mastered this game, add the area code and require players to sort ten digits.
- Instead of numbers, write letters on the cards and ask players to spell out their name.
- Refrigerator magnets with numbers or letters may be used instead of cards.

☀ Some players may find this game easier if an eighth card with a dash is included in their pile.

SKILLS DEVELOPED: Rearranging the cards in the order of the player's home phone number calls on a child's memory, number recognition, and sequencing abilities. Manual dexterity and visual observation also are exercised. An added benefit of this game is that it helps a child remember her home phone number, which can be valuable in an emergency.

THE COVER-UP

PURPOSE: To exercise several different problem-solving skills.

MATERIALS NEEDED: 6 pennies for each player, piece of paper for each player, pen or pencil, 2 dice

NUMBER OF PLAYERS: 2 or more

HOW TO PLAY: Write the numbers one through six on each player's piece of paper. The first player rolls the dice, calls out the numbers he rolled, and places a penny over each of the corresponding numbers on his paper. The next player takes her turn and covers up the numbers rolled. Play continues until one player has covered all the numbers on his paper with pennies.

EXAMPLE: Jackson rolls a three and a four. He places a penny on the 3 and on the 4 on his paper. Cathy rolls a six and a one, so she covers those two numbers on her paper. Mom rolls a four and a four and places a penny on the 4 on her paper. The three continue playing until one player has all numbers covered by pennies.

HINTS AND VARIATIONS

- 🔅 Play with one die instead of two dice.

- 🔅 If a player rolls a number that's already been covered, he does not add another penny to that number.

- 🔅 In the competitive version of this game, the first player to cover all her numbers wins, and she is the first player to roll the die in the next round.

- 🔅 Laminate the strips of paper and tuck them into a plastic sandwich bag with the die and pennies so this game can be played on the go.

- 🔅 If they are able, have the children create their play cards by writing the numbers on their papers themselves.

- 🔅 A more challenging version uses two dice. First, players write the numbers two through twelve on their blank paper. When the dice are rolled, players add the two numbers together and place a penny on the number that represents the sum.

- 🔅 Another challenging variation is to use dominoes instead of dice. Scatter the dominoes facedown in the center of the table. Players take turns selecting one domino and using it to cover up the number that represents the number of dots shown on the domino.

SKILLS DEVELOPED: Determining the numbers rolled on the dice and finding the corresponding numbers on the sheet of paper is a challenging problem-solving activity for preschoolers that involves counting, comparing, and matching. Manual dexterity is also exercised, especially if the children write the numbers on their own papers.

MEASURING UP

PURPOSE: To understand the concept of measurement by measuring and comparing household items, and to exercise visual observation, problem solving, spatial ability, and motor skills.

MATERIALS NEEDED: Ruler, tape measure, or yardstick; several household objects; paper; pens or pencils

NUMBER OF PLAYERS: 1 or more

HOW TO PLAY: First, give the players a lesson on how to take measurements using a ruler, tape measure, or yardstick. Then select one object for each player and ask the players to measure their objects. Have them compare their measurements to determine whose object is taller, wider, or deeper. If there is only one player, assign two objects to her to measure, compare, and determine which is largest.

EXAMPLE: Claire, Jay, and Kelly learned how to take measurements using a yardstick. Then Mom gives them each an object to measure. Claire is assigned a chair, Jay is assigned the front door, and Kelly is assigned the end table. Mom asks them to measure the width of their objects (with help from Mom if needed). While they are measuring, Mom writes the names of the three players on a piece of paper. Next to each name, she writes the name of the object they are assigned to measure.

Claire determines that the chair is 20 inches, Jay says that the door is 36 inches, and Kelly finds that the end table is 18 inches. With help, they write these three numbers on the paper next to their names. As a group, they figure that Jay's door is the widest object. They report their results to Mom. Mom asks them to go back and measure the depth of each of their objects. Again, the children measure their objects, write the numbers on the paper, and compare results to determine that the chair is the deepest object.

HINTS AND VARIATIONS

- In the first round, help players use the ruler to measure their objects.
- Ask the children to record their measurements on a piece of paper, or you may help them by writing down the measurements they call out.
- Take this game outside the home by comparing the size of your table to the size of a table in a restaurant, your chair to the size of the chairs in the pediatrician's office, or your bookshelf to the size of the bookshelves in the library.
- Ask players to predict which object is largest before measuring, and then compare results to the prediction.
- Provide different measurement tools so players may experiment with different devices.
- Draw a picture of each object and label it with its measurements

SKILLS DEVELOPED: Understanding the concept of measurement can be quite a stretch for a preschooler, but this game is a first step toward developing that understanding. Don't expect your child to grasp the concept immediately. An additional complexity is learning how to use a ruler or yardstick. The most complex concept is distinguishing between height, width, and depth. Play this game in stages, and guide the players through each task the first few times you play. Over time the players can become more independent in taking, recording, and comparing measurements. This game employs problem-solving skills in every step and helps children understand spatial relationships.

DICE ROUNDS

PURPOSE: To stimulate problem-solving skills and visual observation by comparing rolls of the dice to determine the high roller.

MATERIALS NEEDED: 2 dice; at least 15 pennies, poker chips, or toothpicks

NUMBER OF PLAYERS: 2 or more

HOW TO PLAY: The players sit in a circle. In the first round, each player takes a turn rolling the dice. That player adds up the numbers on the face of the dice and announces the total. After all players have rolled the dice, the group determines who had the highest roll. That player gets a penny or a poker chip and rolls the dice first in the next round. Play for several rounds, and declare a winner at the end of the game based on who has collected the highest number of pennies or poker chips.

EXAMPLE: Lauren, Audrey, and Beth sit on the floor in a circle. Lauren rolls a two and a six. She calls out "Eight." Next Audrey rolls a three and a two. She calls out "Five." Beth rolls a five and a one. She calls out "Six." Then the three girls compare their sums. They agree that Lauren had the highest roll, so she earns one penny. Lauren starts the next round. The player with the highest sum in that round, Beth, earns a penny. Beth starts the third round. The girls play until all fifteen pennies have been distributed. Then they count the number of pennies that each player has earned.

HINTS AND VARIATIONS

- 🔅 If using dice for the first time, preschool children may find it easier to play with one die instead of two.

- If there is a tie during one round, those two players have a "face off," where each rolls one die, and the player with the highest score wins the round.

- Instead of playing for pennies, play for snacks. The winner in each round earns a jelly bean, a grape, a pretzel, three potato chips, two raisins, or another snack.

- If children have a difficult time remembering their roll at the end of the round, provide each player with pencil and paper to write down their scores.

- For a variation, award the penny or the point to the player with the lowest roll rather than the highest roll.

- A noncompetitive version of this game eliminates the penny reward for the highest roller in each round. Rather, the high-rolling player becomes the first to roll the dice in the next round. No one keeps track of how often each player was the highest roller.

SKILLS DEVELOPED: *Dice Rounds* encourages children to use several different types of problem-solving skills that involve counting, adding, and comparing. For example, viewing the rolled dice and determining how many dots are on each is the first problem-solving skill exercised in this game. After many rounds, preschoolers begin to recognize the layout of the dots and can identify the number on the face of the die without counting each dot.

Adding together the dots on the two dice is the second problem-solving skill practiced in this game. The third is determining which player had the highest number of dots in the round. The fourth problem-solving skill comes into play when it's time to declare a winner if the competitive version of the game is being played. The pennies of each player must be counted and then compared with one another to determine who has the highest number.

SKYSCRAPERS

PURPOSE: To stimulate problem-solving skills and understanding of spatial relationships by using visual observation, experimentation, and motor skills to build a skyscraper out of paper cups.

MATERIALS NEEDED: Box of small paper cups

NUMBER OF PLAYERS: 2 or more

HOW TO PLAY: Split the box of paper cups evenly among the players. If there are four or more players, organize them into teams of two. Ask each team or player to build the highest structure by stacking the paper cups on top of one another in a creative way. Send the teams or players to different rooms so they can't watch the other team. Give the teams five or ten minutes to build their skyscraper, and then compare results.

EXAMPLE: Andrea and Sydney are on one team, and Evan and Jake are on the other team. Each team is given forty small paper cups and is sent to a designated room in the house. The timer is set for ten minutes. Andrea and Sydney arrange a bottom tier of upright cups and carefully stack more tiers on top of it. Meanwhile, Evan and Jake try stacking the first tier in an upright position, the second tier in an upside-down position, and so on. The boys find this structure to be unstable, so they switch to one made entirely of upside-down cups. When the timer rings, the boys' skyscraper is 24 inches tall, and the girls' is 20 inches tall.

HINTS AND VARIATIONS

‑👁‑ Substitute other materials for the small paper cups, such as blocks, straws and clay, sheets of cardboard and cups, dry spaghetti and tape, or toothpicks and paper cups. Providing two or three different materials adds interest and strategy to the game. Just make sure that each team has an equal amount of starting materials.

- After the skyscrapers are built, test their strength by giving each team a weighted object to balance on top, such as a block or a quarter.

- During the game, check on each team or player to make sure that all of them are participating and that the teams are making progress.

- This may be a multiple-round game. After the first round, change the materials by adding another element (such as toothpicks) and perhaps removing half the cups.

- This game does not have to be competitive, and it is not necessary for players to work in separate rooms. In fact, after the first round, the players and teams may want to join forces to build one structure together.

- You may want to forgo using the timer, as this may be a source of pressure.

SKILLS DEVELOPED: *Skyscrapers* allows children to think creatively about how to use given materials to build a structure. When children work in pairs, they also learn about cooperation and teamwork. Children usually experiment with a few different models before deciding on a building approach. This experimentation is a form of problem solving and should be encouraged. This game also draws on motor skills and hand-eye coordination in building the structures.

VIRTUAL SHOPPING

PURPOSE: To exercise visual observation, problem solving, and motor skills by selecting favorite items in catalogs and creating one's own catalog.

MATERIALS NEEDED: Children's magazines and catalogs; scissors (one for each player); glue sticks or glue; paper; markers, crayons, pens, or pencils; play money

NUMBER OF PLAYERS: 1 or more

HOW TO PLAY: Give players a few children's magazines and catalogs and ask them to flip through the pages, identify things they like, and cut them out. The players will create their own one-page catalog using their favorite items. Children glue their cutouts to a piece of paper using a glue stick. They set a dollar price for each item and write the number underneath each picture. Distribute the play money and take them on a virtual shopping trip once their catalogs are complete.

EXAMPLE: Kendra's dad had saved several mail-order catalogs and parenting magazines. Kendra and her friend Tyler look through the material and select the toys and other items that they like. They cut these pictures out with help from Dad and then glue several of the pictures to sheets of paper using a glue stick. Dad helps them write numbers below each item as they decide on a price for each item in their catalogs. After Dad gives them play money, he lets them decide which merchandise they want to buy. Dad then collects the play money accordingly. The children switch catalogs and buy merchandise from each other's catalogs with their remaining play money.

HINTS AND VARIATIONS

- Save old magazines, catalogs, and advertising circulars for activities like this one, especially those with pictures of children and toys. It's a great opportunity for reusing items.
- Children may cut out far more pictures than they end up using. In this case, let them create a multipage catalog or save some pictures for another day.
- To help children set prices, write down several numbers on a piece of paper from which they may choose, for example, 1, 2, 3, 5, 8, 10.

SKILLS DEVELOPED: *Virtual Shopping* teaches about reusing old items, counting, and setting priorities. When looking through catalogs for their favorite items, children stimulate their visual observation skills. Cutting, arranging, and pasting use fine motor skills. Setting prices involves some problem solving, as does the virtual shopping trip, where they dole out play money and pretend to buy merchandise from their catalogs.

GRAPHIC CLOTHES

PURPOSE: To develop problem-solving skills and spatial ability by creating a graph that records the number of clothing pieces the preschooler is wearing.

MATERIALS NEEDED: Paper, pen or pencil, tape, markers or crayons

NUMBER OF PLAYERS: 1 or more

HOW TO PLAY: Create a bar chart on a piece of paper, writing the days of the week along the bottom of the chart and the numbers one through twelve up the left side. Post this chart in your child's bedroom. Each morning before he gets dressed, ask him how many pieces of clothing he thinks he'll be wearing that day, and record that number on the chart. As he gets dressed, have him count the number of articles of clothing that he's putting on and compare this to his prediction. Together, record the number of clothing pieces on the chart by drawing a bar for that day. Your child can color the bar with markers or crayons. Every few days, compare the numbers to past days.

EXAMPLE: Sara and Emily post blank charts in their bedroom on Sunday night. They talk with Mom about which outfits they plan to wear on Monday. Mom asks how many articles of clothing they think they will be wearing once they are completely dressed. Sara predicts seven and Emily predicts nine. Mom records their predictions at the bottom of their charts. On Monday morning, as the girls get dressed, they count the number of articles of clothing they are putting on. Sara wears eight items and Emily wears nine. Mom helps them outline the appropriate number of bars on the "Monday" column in the chart, and then the girls color in their bars.

HINTS AND VARIATIONS

- ☀ You may want to discuss with the children what they will wear the night before as they're getting ready for bed and ask for their predictions at that time. This may help speed the process of getting dressed the next morning. Some parents have found that children enjoy laying out the clothes they will be wearing on the floor in the shape of a child.
- ☀ In addition to comparing actual results to predictions, each child may compare her own results to those of her siblings.
- ☀ Instead of recording the number of articles of clothing that your preschooler is wearing, record the number of minutes it takes him to dress himself. This may encourage children to dress quickly to beat their previous times.

- ✨ You (or your child) may write the predicted numbers at the bottom of the chart, below the days of the week. You may record the actual number just above each daily bar.
- ✨ If you find that mornings are too rushed to do this activity, your child may do it after school or that evening.
- ✨ After your youngster has mastered this game, move on to counting and graphing other things in your daily routine, such as the number of letters you get in the mail. Try to find activities that generate higher numbers.

SKILLS DEVELOPED: Aside from exercising problem-solving skills and teaching graphical representation, this game may give your child the incentive to dress more quickly and independently in the morning. Mentally counting articles of clothing before he's dressed is a stimulating activity, and comparing that number to the actual is enlightening. Predictions tend to get closer to actual results over time.

The chief lesson to be learned here, though, is how to read a bar chart or a graph. Using something that directly applies to your child, such as the clothing she is wearing, helps make the graphing exercise meaningful. The simple numbers in this game also make the overall concept easier to understand.

SHAPE MAKING

PURPOSE: To turn toothpicks into shapes using problem-solving skills, experimentation, creative thinking, and spatial thinking.

MATERIALS NEEDED: Box of toothpicks

NUMBER OF PLAYERS: 2 or more

HOW TO PLAY: Give the players several toothpicks each, and ask each to arrange his toothpicks into two distinct shapes, three distinct shapes, or four distinct shapes. Each player may have a different number of starting toothpicks. Once all players have created the shapes, review the names of the shapes. The players hand the toothpicks back to the adult and play another round.

EXAMPLE: Mom gives six toothpicks to Andy, eight toothpicks to Ben, and nine toothpicks to Holly. She asks each player to arrange his or her toothpicks into two different shapes. Andy arranges his six toothpicks into two triangles. Ben arranges his eight toothpicks into two squares. Holly arranges her nine toothpicks into one triangle and one hexagon. Mom reviews the names of the shapes with the kids and then collects the toothpicks.

In the second round, Mom hands out eleven toothpicks to Andy, twelve to Ben, and ten to Holly. She asks each player to arrange his or her toothpicks into three different shapes. After the second round is completed, the children play several more rounds.

HINTS AND VARIATIONS

- Increase the number of toothpicks and the number of shapes that players must form with each round.
- Toothpicks are an ideal starting tool because they are easy to manipulate and experiment with in order to find the right combination of shapes. When children become proficient at this game, however, challenge them further by giving them only paper and pencil and asking them to draw a certain number of shapes using a given number of lines.
- Players may race against each other to complete their shapes.
- Use toothpicks or other sticks of different lengths to make this game more challenging.

SKILLS DEVELOPED: Experimenting with the arrangement of toothpicks in order to achieve the given number of shapes is a fun and challenging activity for preschool children. This is a problem-solving function, but children must use their spatial abilities in creating the form. Manual dexterity and fine motor skills are also exercised in this game.

SHAPE HUNT

PURPOSE: To use visual observation, problem solving, artistic expression, and motor skills while searching for shapes in magazines and creating a shape collage.

MATERIALS NEEDED: Scissors; paper; bowl; magazines, catalogs, and advertising circulars; glue stick

NUMBER OF PLAYERS: 1 or more

HOW TO PLAY: Help the children cut several shapes out of the paper, such as a circle, square, rectangle, triangle, and oval. Put these shapes into a bowl and blindly draw one out. The selected shape is the object of the Shape Hunt.

Each player receives a magazine, a piece of paper, and a pair of scissors and embarks on the Shape Hunt. Players flip through the magazines, searching for objects in pictures or illustrations that are in the same shape as the selected shape. As matching shapes are spotted, players cut them out and glue them to their paper. Encourage the children to arrange the cutouts in a creative collage. When the paper is filled, players count the number of shapes they collected and write the total at the bottom of the paper, with help if necessary. Save the leftover shapes for the next Shape Hunt.

EXAMPLE: Colleen, Maureen, Brian, and Kevin cut several shapes out of paper and put them into a bowl. Kevin draws the circle out of the bowl. The kids each search through magazines and catalogs for pictures with circles in them. The pictures they cut out include a plate, a clock, a round table, a ball, an orange, a mirror, a lamp, and a globe. They glue these pictures to their papers. Each child counts the number of shapes that appear on her or his page and writes the number at the bottom of the paper. While the kids look on, Dad reviews each finished paper and writes a word under each picture to label it, spelling each word out loud.

HINTS AND VARIATIONS

- Interesting starting materials can add to the fun in this game. Use bright, colorful paper, offer scissors with scalloped or zig-zag edges if you have them, and give kids magazines and catalogs that appeal to children.
- Save your old magazines and catalogs throughout the year for this and other games.
- Children may need help spotting shapes in pictures.
- Assign a different shape to each player.

SKILLS DEVELOPED: Searching for shapes in magazines relies on two thought processes. First, visual observation is called into play as children study the pictures. Second, as each picture is examined and identified, the child is using problem-solving skills.

Using the scissors to cut out the pictures and the glue stick to create a collage relies on fine motor skills, and the art of arranging the pictures in the collage is a form of artistic expression. This game's emphasis on shapes can be broadened to other areas by counting the number of shapes and labeling the cutouts with words.

WHAT'S DIFFERENT?

PURPOSE: To use visual observation, memory, and problem-solving skills to determine what has changed in a room in their home.

MATERIALS NEEDED: None

NUMBER OF PLAYERS: 2 or more

HOW TO PLAY: Have the players stay in one room. Go to another room and change or move one object. For example, a picture frame may be turned upside down, or a stuffed animal may be seated in a chair. When you are finished, call the players into the room. Tell them to look around, try to spot the change, and call it out once it's been identified. Play several rounds.

EXAMPLE: Dad, Grace, and Billy decide to use the living room to play *What's Different*. Grace and Billy go into the kitchen while Dad makes a change to the living room. He moves a green pillow from the couch to the rocking chair. Dad calls Billy and Grace into the room. After a few minutes, Grace spots the out-of-place pillow and calls it out. Dad sends the kids out of the room again and places a videotape on the windowsill. The kids are called back in, and this time Billy spots the videotape. After a few more turns, the kids decide to play on their own. Billy moves an object when Grace is out of the room, and after Grace spies it, she takes a turn.

HINTS AND VARIATIONS

- Begin with obvious changes and make them subtler in subsequent rounds.
- This game works best when an adult makes the room changes for the first few rounds, so he can demonstrate the kinds of changes that are appropriate.

🔅 Rather than playing several rounds in succession, play one round each day at the same time, such as when your preschooler wakes up or when he comes home from school or day care.

🔅 When "lookers" are stumped, the player who made the change may use the words *hot, cold, warm,* and *cool* to provide hints.

🔅 Once the kids are proficient players, alternate turns. In each round, the player who first identifies the change in the room becomes the player who makes the room change in the next round.

SKILLS DEVELOPED: When this game is played, adults are often amazed at how much detailed information children have stored in their minds and how accurate their memories are. This is a challenging game that kids of all ages love. As they look around a room for the changes, children use visual observation skills as well as memory and problem-solving skills. As they eye different objects, they ask themselves whether it is in a new position or not. This is a problem-solving skill, and as children become more proficient, they will be able to process this self-imposed question more quickly.

DETECTIVE MEMORY

PURPOSE: To use observation skills, problem solving, and short-term memory while recalling objects on a tray.

MATERIALS NEEDED: Assorted household objects (key, postage stamp, baby sock, raisin, pen, spool of thread, rubber band, nail, bracelet, napkin, small toy, or others); large tray; cloth or towel; paper; pen or pencil

NUMBER OF PLAYERS: 2 or more

HOW TO PLAY: Place ten household objects on a large tray and cover it with a cloth or towel. Sample objects are a paper clip, a spoon, a photo, a quarter, and a crayon. Ask the players to gather around. Remove the cover and have the players take turns naming one object they see on the tray. When all objects have been named, remove the tray.

Ask the players to name the objects that were on the tray. Write down the objects that are recalled and give clues for the objects that are not recalled. Bring the tray back and have the group identify the objects they forgot. Play a few times with a different set of objects in each round.

EXAMPLE: Mom places ten household objects on a large tray and covers it with a towel. Megan, Jack, and Kaitlin sit on the floor in a circle. Mom places the tray on the floor in the middle of the circle and removes the towel. The three players rotate around the circle, naming objects they see on the tray. Megan says "Sock." Jack says "Nail." Kaitlin says "Picture." They continue until all ten objects have been named.

Mom removes the tray and returns with paper and pencil. The children call out objects they remember from the tray. Once they name seven objects, they can't remember any more. Mom gives a few clues and they name two more objects. Then Mom brings the tray back, and the kids recognize and call out the tenth object.

HINTS AND VARIATIONS

- When the tray is first uncovered for the children, ask them to call out the objects on the tray one at a time to help them remember its contents. With more experienced players, ask them to study the objects silently.

- A competitive version of this game has children rotating around the circle when it's time to recall the objects on the tray. They take turns, naming objects one at a time. The last player to remember an object wins the round.

- For older children, hand out paper and pencils to all players and ask them to write down the name of all the objects from the tray that they can remember. Compare lists and see who remembered the highest number of objects.

SKILLS DEVELOPED: This is a fun brain-teasing game for children and adults. It's more difficult than you expect to recall ten items on a tray. Preschool children enjoy the challenge. This game is also flexible, so you can impose structure or not, depending on the playing style of the children. The key thinking process is short-term memory. Children must also use their visual observation skills to carefully study all the objects on the tray.

HUCKLE BUCKLE BEANSTALK

PURPOSE: To exercise problem-solving skills by hiding a small toy and then relying on keen observation skills to find it.

MATERIALS NEEDED: Small toy, about 2 to 3 inches long or wide

NUMBER OF PLAYERS: 2 or more

HOW TO PLAY: Designate a room in which to play the game. In each round, one child plays the role of the "hider" and all the other players are the "finders." To begin, all the players except the hider leave the designated room. Without moving any other objects, the hider hides the small toy in a location that is visible but not too obvious. Unacceptable hiding spots include: under a pillow, inside a drawer, at the bottom of a wastebasket, or behind a couch. Acceptable hiding spots include: on a bookshelf, on a windowsill, next to a lamp, or hanging over a picture frame. Once the toy is hidden, the hider invites the finders back into the room. They must hold their hands behind their backs as they walk around the room searching for the hidden toy. They cannot touch or move anything as they search. When the toy is spotted, the player calls out "Huckle Buckle Beanstalk!" and retrieves the toy. In the next round, that player is the hider. Continue playing for several rounds, alternating hiders based on who found the toy in the previous round.

EXAMPLE: Bobby, Rebecca, and Zack decide to use a miniature rubber duck as the object in *Huckle Buckle Beanstalk*. Bobby and Rebecca leave the room while Zack hides the duck. He places it on the floor next to a large piece of furniture. When Bobby and Rebecca return, they search for a few minutes. Bobby spots it and yells "Huckle Buckle Beanstalk!"

Now Bobby is the hider. Rebecca and Zack leave the room while Bobby sits the duck on top of a picture frame. When the finders return, they spend several minutes looking. Bobby decides to give them clues, telling them when they are "hot" (close) or "cold" (far away). Finally Rebecca finds the duck.

HINTS AND VARIATIONS

- An adult should play with the children in the first few rounds, and stay close by to help facilitate the game in later rounds. Older children can play without adult assistance.
- When the finders are stumped, the hider may give clues by telling them when they are "hot" or "cold."
- Make sure all players understand that the toy must be visible and that nothing should be moved. This game can be frustrating if players are forced to search through closets, cabinets, or drawers. Explain that the finders must search with their hands behind their backs.

SKILLS DEVELOPED: In *Huckle Buckle Beanstalk,* children learn to look at a room in a whole new way when they are playing the role of the hider. They learn to be strategic and creative in selecting hiding spots. When playing the role of finder, the children also look at the room in a whole new way, noticing things that they never noticed before as they sharpen their visual observation skills searching for the hidden object. Children love searching for and finding the hidden toy and will play round after round without tiring. This game has no natural ending and no final winners or losers—everyone gets a turn to hide the toy once she finds it.

MENU MAKER

PURPOSE: To use visual observation, problem solving, imagination, and motor skills in creating a restaurant menu and assigning prices.

MATERIALS NEEDED: Paper; old magazines and grocery store circulars; scissors; glue stick or tape; marker, crayon, or pencil; play money

NUMBER OF PLAYERS: 1 or more

HOW TO PLAY: Fold a sheet of paper in half for each player. These are the menus. Give the players old magazines and grocery store circulars to search for pictures of foods they like. Players cut out pictures of their favorite foods and use a glue stick or tape to attach the clippings to the folded pieces of paper. With an adult's help, players write the first letter of each food underneath the photo. Players also set a price for each food in dollars and write this number under each photo. Once the menus are complete, the players receive play money and pretend to order food from the menus. An adult or older child takes the orders and gives each player a bill. Players pay the bill with their play money.

EXAMPLE: Samantha and Charlie flip through magazines and grocery store circulars and cut out several pictures of food. Next they glue their food clippings to their menus. Samantha glues pictures of Oreos, broccoli, apples, hot dogs, and french fries. Charlie attaches clippings of cereal, bananas, waffles, juice, and pudding. Dad helps the children identify the starting letter for each food, and they write the letters under each photo.

Dad writes the numbers one through ten on a piece of paper and tells the kids that they can select any of these numbers as a price. As they set the prices, Dad helps them write these numbers under each photo.

Dad gives each of them twenty dollars in play money. He takes notes as Samantha and Charlie order food off the menu. Dad presents Samantha with a bill for twelve dollars. Samantha counts out twelve dollars. Charlie pays his bill for eight dollars.

HINTS AND VARIATIONS

- Instead of clippings, children may draw pictures of their favorite foods on their menus.
- Encourage players to select a variety of foods to include on their menus, including some healthy choices.
- Adults or children may write the entire word as a label under each menu item.
- The two distinct activities of this game may be broken up into two days. On the first day, create the menu. On the second day, order off the menu.

SKILLS DEVELOPED: In *Menu Maker*, children get the opportunity to be creative in developing a menu of foods they love. They don't need to be restricted to pictures they find in magazines and advertising circulars; they may supplement with hand-drawn pictures. The process of putting together the menu, which involves cutting, arranging, and pasting, stimulates fine motor skills. Writing beginning word sounds and prices under each food stimulates problem-solving skills. Players engage in imaginative play as they order food off their own menus and pay their bills.

TASTE TEST

PURPOSE: To identify flavors using the sense of taste.

MATERIALS NEEDED: Variety of foods with different tastes, such as flavored jelly beans

NUMBER OF PLAYERS: 1 or more

HOW TO PLAY: Buy jelly beans with unique flavors for each color, or use other foods with a variety of flavors. Ask players to close their eyes and then pop a jelly bean into their open mouths. Each player should receive the same flavor. Have players remain silent until all have had a chance to chew their jelly beans. Then count to three, and on the count of three, ask players to guess the flavor of their candies. Compare guesses, and then reveal the correct flavor.

EXAMPLE: Mom buys ten flavors of jelly beans (watermelon, root beer, coconut, pineapple, chocolate, strawberry, blueberry, banana, apple, and lime). Sedona and Nolan close their eyes and open their mouths. Mom pops a watermelon-flavored jelly bean in each player's mouth and eats one herself. The players chew silently, and then Mom says, "On the count of three, call out your guess for the flavor of this jelly bean. One, two, three!"

Sedona says "Strawberry!" Nolan says "Cherry!" Mom tells them that it was watermelon. They try again with another flavor, and play several rounds until the jelly beans are gone.

HINTS AND VARIATIONS

- Jelly beans are ideal for this game, since they are small, have strong flavors and consistent texture, and often don't have a strong scent.

- If you are opposed to using jelly beans, this game may be played with juice (apple juice, orange juice, grape juice, cran-raspberry juice), cut fruit (bananas, strawberries, grapes, watermelon, honeydew melon, cantaloupe, raspberries, blueberries), or other foods or drinks. However, these are less challenging, since players can use texture and scent as clues to determine the flavor.

- If you use foods other than jelly beans, ask players to close their eyes and pinch their noses closed when tasting the food so they can't rely on their sense of smell to identify the flavor.

- Flavored jelly beans can often be found at candy stores.

- Experiment with different ways of blindfolding the children (blindfolds versus closed eyes) and distributing the food (popping into their mouths versus putting it in their hands). Some players can't resist peeking!

- Incorporate two different jelly bean flavors with the same color. For example use two green jelly beans—green apple and lime, two red—cinnamon and raspberry, and two yellow—banana and pineapple. Give players the matching pair of jelly beans and ask them to distinguish the flavors.

- Make this game competitive by keeping track of how many times each player correctly identifies the flavor. Give players a penny for each correct guess, and at the end of the game have the players count their pennies.

SKILLS DEVELOPED: *Taste Test* gives players the opportunity to focus on gathering information from just one sense: their sense of taste. Giving children plenty of time to chew and taste their samples helps them appreciate and understand their ability to identify unique tastes. If the competitive version of this game is played, children also use problem-solving skills to count the number of correct flavors they identified.

SNIFF TEST

PURPOSE: To identify scents using the sense of smell.

MATERIALS NEEDED: Variety of items with unique scents, paper cups, cheesecloth, rubber bands, paper, pen or pencil

NUMBER OF PLAYERS: 1 or more

HOW TO PLAY: Gather eight items with pungent smells. Put each item in a paper cup. Cut the cheesecloth into large squares and cover each cup to allow the scent to come through. Secure each cheesecloth with a rubber band. Number each cup and give each participant a piece of paper with corresponding numbers so you can help them record their answers.

Each player takes a cup, sniffs it, and tries to identify the object. Write (or help the child write) his answer on his paper. Then the cups are passed to another player. Players continue sniffing until they have sampled all the cups and have a guess written next to each number on their paper.

One by one, reveal the contents of each cup by removing the cheesecloth. Players may want to sniff them again. Compare guesses with the actual items.

EXAMPLE: For Melissa's birthday party, Mom and Dad place pungent items in each of six paper cups. At the party, the five guests and Melissa each receive a piece of paper and one cup to sniff. Once they make a guess, they relay it to an adult, who records it on their paper for them. Then the players rotate the cups and each player sniffs another one. Guesses are recorded and the cups are rotated again. Play continues until all players have guesses for all six cups.

Dad reveals the contents of the first cup, a slice of banana. Four of the guests had correctly identified this, and the other two had guessed pineapple and vanilla cake. Dad reveals the contents of the second cup, shampoo. Two of the guests had correctly identified this. Dad continues revealing the contents of each cup one by one, and players share their guesses with one another.

HINTS AND VARIATIONS

- Suggested items with pungent smells include: orange slice, suntan lotion, banana, cinnamon, flower, chocolate, shampoo, and onion.
- To make things more challenging, place something with a neutral smell in one cup, such as water or a cotton ball.
- The competitive version of this game has players counting the number of correct answers they had at the end of the game.

SKILLS DEVELOPED: *Sniff Test* gives players the opportunity to focus on gathering information from just one sense: their sense of smell. Comparing actual answers to guesses is a fun activity, and if the competitive version of this game is played, children also use problem-solving skills to count the number of correct scents they identified.

TOUCH POINTS

PURPOSE: To identify objects using the sense of touch.

MATERIALS NEEDED: Variety of small objects that fit inside a tissue box; empty tissue box

NUMBER OF PLAYERS: 1 or more

HOW TO PLAY: Gather five to ten objects with unique textures or shapes, such as a cotton ball and a small straw. Place one object inside an empty square-shaped tissue box and hide the others.

Players sit in a circle. Pass the tissue box around the circle. One at a time, without looking in the box, players silently reach into the tissue box and feel the object. Once everyone has had a chance to feel the object, count to three and all players simultaneously call out their guesses. Take out the object and show it to all the players. Compare guesses to the actual object. Repeat the process for each item.

EXAMPLE: Dad gathers six items. He puts the first item, a dime, into an empty tissue box. Olivia feels the object first, followed by Jameson. Dad counts to three, and Olivia and Jameson simultaneously call out their guesses. Olivia says "Penny!" and Jameson guesses "Dime!" Dad pulls out the dime and shows it to the children, who compare it to their guesses. Next Dad puts a Cheerio in the box. This time Jameson touches it first, followed by Olivia. Dad counts to three. Olivia guesses "Froot Loop!" and Jameson guesses "Cheerio!" Dad reveals the object. They continue playing this game for all six objects Dad had gathered.

HINTS AND VARIATIONS

- Suggested items include: grape, cotton, paper clip, coin, key, marble or small ball, piece of aluminum foil, photo, jelly bean, straw, crayon, children's scissors, piece of tape, and mint candy.

- Rather than pulling objects out of a tissue box, try using a sock. It may be more difficult to insert the object, but children aren't able to peek.
- The competitive version of this game has players counting the number of correct answers they have throughout the game. Players may earn a penny or other token for every correct answer. At the end of the game, players count the number of pennies they earned.

SKILLS DEVELOPED: *Touch Points* gives players the opportunity to focus on gathering information from just one isolated sense: their sense of touch. Players should not be allowed to gather any other clues by looking at the object, smelling it, or listening to the way it sounds when the box is shaken. If the competitive version of this game is played, children also use problem-solving skills to count the number of items they correctly identified throughout the game.

FREEZE-FRAME

PURPOSE: To use auditory clues to express oneself through dance and then freeze in place.

MATERIALS NEEDED: Lively music, tape or CD player

NUMBER OF PLAYERS: 1 or more

HOW TO PLAY: Turn on the music and have the players dance. When the volume is turned up, tell players to dance rapidly with large, exaggerated movements. When the volume is turned down, encourage players to dance slowly with small, delicate, and light movements. When the music stops altogether, tell the players to freeze in place. Players try to hold their freeze position as long as possible. The last player to move wins the round.

EXAMPLE: Mom plays the song "Under the Sea" from *The Little Mermaid*. Sarah, Jordan, and Abigail dance to the music. When Mom turns the volume up, they swing their arms and dance wildly. When Mom turns the volume down, they dance on their tiptoes, swaying their arms through the air, imitating ballerinas. When Mom stops the music altogether, all three players freeze in place. Abigail is the first to move, and then Sarah. Jordan stays completely still the longest, so she wins the round. Then Mom plays another song for the next round.

HINTS AND VARIATIONS

- 🔆 Lively, familiar music inspires the most creative dancing. The adult may join in the dancing periodically.
- 🔆 As players are eliminated from the game, they may make silly faces at the remaining frozen players in an attempt to make them laugh and move.
- 🔆 Rather than have movements change from big to small as the volume of the music decreases, designate one end of the room as the "soft" end and another as the "loud" end. As the volume increases or decreases, players must dance toward the appropriate end of the room.

SKILLS DEVELOPED: *Freeze-Frame* is an active game that challenges players to gather auditory information to regulate their body movements. The varied dancing and freezing allows children to express themselves through dance and exercises their gross motor skills. Players must also process information about the volume of the music and translate that into a dancing style throughout the game. Making the connection between what they hear and how they move their bodies is a challenging directive that becomes easier with practice.

HAND PUZZLE

PURPOSE: To exercise artistic expression by creating a hand puzzle and using problem-solving skills to put it together.

MATERIALS NEEDED: Crayons and markers, heavyweight paper or cardboard (white or light colored), scissors, glue stick or tape, colored paper

NUMBER OF PLAYERS: 1 or more

HOW TO PLAY: Players begin by tracing the outline of their hands onto the heavyweight paper. Once the outline is complete, players color the area inside their hand outlines. Encourage players to use a variety of colors and designs. Once the coloring is complete, players cut out their hands, then cut the hands themselves into several small pieces. The pieces are shuffled, and players try to reassemble their hands by putting the pieces back together. Once the hands have been reassembled, players may glue the assembled pieces to a colored piece of paper using a glue stick or tape.

EXAMPLE: Justin and Owen each outline their hands on a piece of white paper using a black marker. Then they color the inside of the hands. Each player also puts a sticker inside his hand drawing. Then the boys cut out their hands. Justin cuts his hand into twelve pieces and Owen cuts his into eight. Mom gives each player a piece of bright red paper. Justin and Owen reassemble their hands on the red paper, and then glue the pieces in place. They each write their name on the bottom of the paper.

HINTS AND VARIATIONS

- Young players may need assistance in drawing the outline of their hands. They may also need help in cutting around the outline of the hands. Encourage children to cut the hands into pieces by themselves regardless of their cutting abilities.

- The hands should be cut into at least five pieces, but no more than fifteen. More patient players will be able to handle a larger number of puzzle pieces.

- Use heavyweight white paper or cardboard for the hand design if you have it, because it will be easier to piece back together once it's been cut.

- Give players a sticker to place inside their hand drawings before cutting.

- The competitive version of this game has players racing against each other to put their hand puzzles together.

- Instead of coloring the hands with crayons or markers, opt for a more involved piece of art. Give children white glue, paintbrushes, and colorful tissue-paper squares. Encourage children to glue tissue paper to the white paper, layering squares of tissue paper on top of one another. Wait a day for the glue to dry, and then outline the child's hand over the tissue-paper collage. Cut out the hand and continue playing.

SKILLS DEVELOPED: This is a quiet game that begins with artistic expression as children create unique artwork. Using scissors to cut out the hands stimulates fine motor skills. Players then shift gears to a problem-solving mode for the final segment, where they must fit the puzzle pieces together. Mounting the reassembled hand onto a piece of paper leaves children with a lasting piece of art.

MISSING LETTERS

PURPOSE: To use visual and problem-solving skills to determine which letter in a word is missing.

MATERIALS NEEDED: Paper, pen or pencil, magnetic wood or plastic letters

NUMBER OF PLAYERS: 1 or more

HOW TO PLAY: Write a simple word on the piece of paper and show it to the children. Use the magnetic letters to spell out the word, but leave one letter out. Players find the missing magnetic letter and put it in place. If two or more players are participating, have them take turns trying to complete the word.

EXAMPLE: Dad writes SUN on a piece of paper. He asks Katie and Peter if they know the word, and neither player does. He tells them what the word is. He then uses magnetic letters to spell S __ N on the refrigerator. Dad asks Katie to fill in the missing letter. Katie refers to the word on the paper to determine that the letter U is missing. She finds the letter and places it on the refrigerator in the correct position.

Next Dad writes DOG. Peter is familiar with the word. Dad spells DO__ with the magnetic letters. Peter finds the G and puts it at the end of the word.

HINTS AND VARIATIONS
- For prereaders, select very simple three-letter words. You may even start with the player's first name. More advanced children may receive more difficult words.
- Once advanced players are familiar with this game, have the players rely more on their memory. Write down the word, discuss it, and then hide the paper. Use the magnetic letters to spell

out the word, leaving a letter out, and see if players can recall the spelling of the word without referring to the paper.

- Another variation for more advanced players is to leave out two letters.
- To get children accustomed to seeing lowercase letters, initially write the word in lowercase letters.
- This game may be played in the bathtub with foam letters.
- Rather than use magnetic letters, write the same word twice, once with a letter missing, and ask the player to write in the missing letter.
- The competitive version of this game has players racing against each other to complete words that they receive simultaneously. Or, players may earn a penny or a token for each completed word, and count their tokens at the end of the game.

SKILLS DEVELOPED: *Missing Letters* is great for children who have mastered the ability to identify beginning sounds and ending sounds of words. This game gets them thinking about the sounds in the middle of words. Players use their problem-solving skills to compare the written word with the magnetic word and determine which letter is missing. Players also use their visual observation skills as they search for the missing letter.

HIGH CARD

PURPOSE: To exercise visual observation and problem-solving skills to compare numbers on playing cards.

MATERIALS NEEDED: Deck of cards

NUMBER OF PLAYERS: 2 or more

HOW TO PLAY: Remove the face cards and aces from the deck of cards. Split the remaining cards evenly among all the players, and have the players stack their cards facedown in front of them. In the first round, the youngest player turns over the top card, and other players do the same, rotating clockwise. The player with the highest card wins all the cards that have been turned over in that round. However, if a player turns over a card with a number that is equal to her age, she keeps that card. Players keep the cards that they win in a separate pile.

In the next round, the player who won the most cards in the previous round turns over the first card, and others follow in a clockwise fashion. Again, the player with the highest card wins all the cards from this round, and any player who turns over a card equal to his age keeps that card.

Continue until all the cards have been played. Each player counts the number of cards she won, and the player with the most cards is declared the winner. This player may start the first round in the next game.

EXAMPLE: Dad removes all the face cards and aces from the deck and deals the remaining cards to Lauren, Sam, and himself. The players stack their cards facedown in front of them. Since Sam is the youngest, he turns over the first card. It is a 6. Lauren turns over an 8, and Dad turns over a 3. Dad asks who has the highest card, and Lauren answers "I do!" Lauren takes all three cards and piles them faceup.

In the next round, Lauren turns over the first card. Her card is a 4. Sam turns over a 3, and Dad turns over a 6. Dad asks who has the highest card, and Sam and Lauren say "You do!" Sam points out that he turned over a 3 and he is three years old, so he keeps his card and Dad takes the other two.

The group continues playing until all the cards have been played. Then the players count their faceup piles to determine the winner.

HINTS AND VARIATIONS

- If there is a tie between the highest cards, the person whose age is closest to the number on the card wins the round. If that is also a tie, leave the pile in the center and the winner of the next round wins the extra cards.

- To help players distinguish between their playing pile of cards and their pile of cards that they won, they may keep winning cards in a faceup position.

- Once players become familiar with this game, suggest that all players turn over their cards simultaneously in each round, rather than one at a time.

- For more advanced players, add face cards and aces to the game after explaining the sequence: face cards equal 10 each, aces equal 11 (or 1).

SKILLS DEVELOPED: Comparing cards and determining which is highest is a problem-solving skill that helps children understand the relationship among numbers. The competitive nature of this game makes it enjoyable and engaging. In time, children learn to be optimistic when they turn over a high card and pessimistic when they turn over a low card. Determining the winner at the end of the game gives children practice in counting and comparing numbers.

CARNIVAL TOSS

PURPOSE: To use problem solving to keep score by tossing beanbags at targets.

MATERIALS NEEDED: Bowls, pans, pie plates; paper and pencil; yardstick; beanbags or beanbag animals; pennies

NUMBER OF PLAYERS: 1 or more

HOW TO PLAY: Before the game, set up the beanbag targets by laying the bowls, pie plates, and pans on the floor. Each target is assigned a value of one, two, or three points, depending on difficulty (the smaller targets and the farther targets should be worth more points). The point assignments are written on slips of paper, and the papers are placed inside the targets or in front of them. A yardstick is placed a few feet behind the targets.

Each player is given three beanbags. Players stand behind the yardstick and try to toss their beanbags into the targets. At the end of their turn, players count their points earned and receive one penny for every point. Once all players have taken a turn, players compare pennies to see which player earned the highest number of points. That player takes the first turn in the next round.

EXAMPLE: Dad arranges two pie plates, three large bowls, and one small bowl on the floor. He decides that the small bowl is worth three points, one large bowl is worth two points, and all other targets are worth one point. He writes these points on slips of paper and places them inside each target.

Jon and Elizabeth line up behind the yardstick. Jon is given three beanbags and tosses one into the two-point target and one into a one-point target. The third lands on the floor. Dad asks how many points he earned, and he says "Three." Dad gives Jon three pennies. Elizabeth is given three beanbags. She tosses all three into one-point targets. Dad asks how many points she earned, and she answers "Three." Dad gives her three pennies. Then Dad asks the players who earned more pennies. Jon points out that they each have three pennies, so it is a tie.

They play several more rounds, adding more pennies to their collection with each round.

HINTS AND VARIATIONS

- To avoid discouragement, move the yardstick closer to the targets when younger players take their turn. You may even set a rule that for every year in a player's age, the yardstick is placed one foot farther from the targets. A three-year-old would stand three feet behind the targets, and a six-year-old would stand six feet behind the targets.
- Masking tape may be used instead of a yardstick.
- Encourage the children to tally up their points and pennies without help.
- Experiment with varying the number of beanbags and targets.
- As players become more advanced, increase the number of points on the targets.

SKILLS DEVELOPED: Tossing beanbags into the targets helps children develop their gross motor skills. Tallying up the number of points that they earn in each round is a counting exercise that relies on problem-solving skills. Receiving one penny for each point teaches them about representation. The pennies may become a tool for counting and adding as the counts get higher. Comparing scores is another problem-solving exercise.

NUMBER PUZZLES

PURPOSE: To create hand-drawn puzzles and use counting skills to match the pieces together.

MATERIALS NEEDED: Scissors, paper (preferably construction paper or other heavyweight paper), crayons or markers

NUMBER OF PLAYERS: 1 or more

HOW TO PLAY: Cut the construction paper into twelve pieces and write a number from one to twelve at the top of each piece. Have the children draw a corresponding number of objects (such as circles, lines, happy faces, or worms) on the bottom of each piece of paper. Cut each piece in half so that the number is on one half and the drawing is on the other half.

Shuffle the squares and lay the numbers facedown in one row and the drawings faceup in a row beneath it. Players take turns selecting a number from the top row and finding the matching drawing. If they are successful in picking up the matching piece on the first try, then they keep both pieces. If they are not, then they return the number, and the next player takes his turn. Once all numbers have been selected and matched, players count the number of pieces of paper they have.

EXAMPLE: Mom cuts twelve squares out of construction paper. Bianca writes the numbers from one to twelve at the top of each square. Below the number one, Brandon draws a sun. Below the number two, Bianca draws two people.

Bianca and Brandon help Mom cut each square in half. They make squiggly cut lines rather than straight ones. Then the children arrange the number halves in one row and the pictures in another row.

Brandon goes first. He selects the number two and finds the picture of two people. He matches the pieces. It is clear that they fit together, so he keeps them. Next, Bianca selects the number five and matches it to the picture with five triangles. Brandon chooses the number six and matches it to four circles. The pieces do not fit together, so he returns them to their respective rows.

The children continue playing until all pieces have been matched up. Then they count the number of pieces they have won.

HINTS AND VARIATIONS

- Using squiggly cut lines will help the kids determine when two pieces truly match each other.

- Save the pieces to play at another time. You may even put them in a resealable bag and bring them with you to play outside the home.

- If each piece has a unique color or drawing, children will begin to memorize the matches rather than count the objects and find the corresponding number. Similar drawings and a consistent paper color will discourage this if you think it may become a problem.

SKILLS DEVELOPED: The two segments of this thinking game use different sets of skills. In the first segment, where children create the puzzle pieces, they use their imaginations, fine motor skills, and artistic expression to draw pictures that correspond with the numbers. This is a natural lead-in to the second segment, where children play the game by matching up numbers with pictures and use their problem-solving skills and visual observation skills.

ALPHABET DRAWINGS

PURPOSE: To use critical thinking and imagination to draw pictures of words beginning with a particular letter.

MATERIALS NEEDED: Paper, crayons or markers

NUMBER OF PLAYERS: 1 or more

HOW TO PLAY: The youngest player selects a letter of the alphabet. Players then have a brainstorming session to think of as many words as they can that begin with that letter. Paper and crayons are passed out, and players are challenged to draw five or more illustrations of words that begin with the letter. Players may be given a specific time frame, such as ten minutes. When time is up, select another letter and play again.

EXAMPLE: Stephen selects B. Stephen, Christine, and Mom brainstorm words that begin with B: bat, ball, basement, box, balloon, bread, bump, baseball, basketball, bright, Brian, brown, blue, black, bracelet, Barbie, Barney, bottle, baby. Mom hands out paper and crayons and sets the timer for ten minutes. When time is up, Stephen has drawn five pictures: a baseball, a bat, a balloon, a baby, and the color blue. Christine has drawn five pictures, too: the color blue, the color black, ball, box, and Brian. Christine selects the letter C for the next round.

HINTS AND VARIATIONS

- Give the children more time or less time depending on their ability to draw quickly.
- After the pictures have been drawn, review them with the players and help them spell out a word next to each picture to label that picture. If players are unable to do this, write the words for them.
- To select a letter, have one of the children blindly draw a magnetic letter out of a bowl.
- Challenge the players to draw *at least* five pictures, and more if they have time.
- Make this game competitive by asking players to draw as many pictures as they can within the specified time frame. The player who draws the most pictures wins.
- Ask advanced players to illustrate words that *end* with a particular letter of the alphabet.
- Eliminate the time limit and give players unlimited time to draw five pictures.

SKILLS DEVELOPED: *Alphabet Drawings* takes simple alphabet games one step further. Children must think critically to come up with several words that begin with a particular letter of the alphabet. Generating the ideas is challenging; the initial brainstorming session gives players some ideas. Selecting the words and drawing pictures for each one is an activity that requires players to use their imaginations and express themselves artistically.

DOMINO CONTEST

PURPOSE: To use visual observation and problem-solving skills to count numbers on dominoes and compare dominoes.

MATERIALS NEEDED: Dominoes

NUMBER OF PLAYERS: 2 or more

HOW TO PLAY: Lay the set of dominoes facedown. Each round begins with all players selecting one domino. The first player reveals his domino, names the number of dots on each side, and counts up the total number of all the dots. Each of the other players does the same. Then ask which player has the highest number of dots. The player with the most dots wins the round and collects all the dominoes.

Each player keeps his own dominoes in a pile. After all the facedown dominoes are gone, the players count the dominoes that they've won. The player with the highest number wins the game and goes first in the next game.

EXAMPLE: PJ, Jimmy, and Mom spread several dominoes facedown on a table. They each select one domino. PJ reveals his domino first.

It has two dots on one side and three dots on the other. He says, "Two dots plus three dots equals . . ." He stops to count the dots and continues, "Five. I have five dots."

Jimmy is next. His domino has six dots on one side and four dots on the other. Jimmy says, "Six plus four equals nine. I have nine dots." Mom suggests that he count again. Jimmy says he has ten dots.

Mom's domino has three dots on one side and four on the other. She says, "Three plus four equals seven. I have seven dots." Then Mom asks, "Who has the most dots on their domino?"

After reviewing how many dots each player has, Jimmy and PJ conclude that Jimmy has the most dots in this round. Jimmy collects all three dominoes and starts his own pile. All three players select new dominoes and start a new round. They continue playing until all the dominoes have been taken. Then they count the number of dominoes each player has in his pile to determine the overall winner.

HINTS AND VARIATIONS

- Even though players state the sum in the form of an equation, they will probably need to count the dots on the dominoes to determine the sum.
- Review the sum of each domino at the end of each round to help players determine which player has the highest number of dots.

SKILLS DEVELOPED: *Domino Contest* is a competitive game that's enjoyable for preschoolers. The prospect of winning the round motivates players to add their two numbers together. This counting or addition step is the most challenging segment of the game. Asking players to state their answer in the form of an equation ensures that they look at their domino as two distinct halves, not just one whole, elevating this exercise from simple counting to addition.

At the end of each round, players use their problem-solving skills to compare sums. At the end of the game, players use simple counting skills again to determine how many dominoes they've collected and problem-solving skills to compare these totals and determine an overall winner.

MONEY HUNT

PURPOSE: To stimulate visual observation skills by searching for coins, and problem-solving skills by totaling the finds.

MATERIALS NEEDED: Pennies and nickels

NUMBER OF PLAYERS: 1 or more

HOW TO PLAY: Hide pennies and nickels on windowsills throughout your home. Players race from room to room to find the money. They trade in their nickels for five pennies each, then count the total number of pennies they collected. The player with the most money wins and hides the coins for the next round.

EXAMPLE: Mom hides several pennies and nickels on windowsills throughout the house. She gives Hannah and Eric each a paper cup to collect the coins. The children race from room to room, picking up coins and dropping them in their cups. They return to the kitchen and dump their coins on the table.

Mom asks how many coins each player has. Hannah answers "Eight" and Eric says "Eleven." Mom offers to give them five pennies for each nickel. Hannah trades her two nickels for ten pennies, and Eric trades his one nickel for five pennies.

Mom asks again how many coins each player has. "Sixteen," says Hannah. "Fifteen," says Eric. Since Hannah has the highest number, she wins the round and hides the coins on the windowsills for the next round.

HINTS AND VARIATIONS

- For beginners, you may prefer to play with pennies only.
- For advanced players, you may use pennies, nickels, and dimes.
- Hide the pennies on the windowsills by covering them with small pieces of paper, small cups, silverware, and so on. This makes it more challenging and time consuming to find and collect the coins.

SKILLS DEVELOPED: *Money Hunt* is another competitive game that stimulates early math skills. Teaching children that five pennies equals one nickel is an important yet difficult concept. Hunting for money is the exciting segment of this game. It is interesting to see their reaction to trading in their nickels for pennies.

The skills used in this game are visual observation during the hunt itself and problem-solving skills to count the pennies and determine who has the highest number.

BEANBAG BALANCE

PURPOSE: To stimulate visual observation, imagination, and gross motor skills in a balancing game.

MATERIALS NEEDED: Beanbags or beanbag animals, paper and pencil (optional)

NUMBER OF PLAYERS: 2 or more

HOW TO PLAY: Establish a starting line and a finish line. The first player balances a beanbag on his body as he makes his way from the starting line to the finish line. The bag may be positioned on any part of the body, such as the head, neck, arm, or shoulder, and the child may travel in any manner he chooses, such as hop, skip, walk, or crawl. The goal is to make it to the finish line without dropping the beanbag.

The other players must follow the first player's challenge and carry their beanbags from start to finish in the same manner. Each player who makes it to the finish line without dropping her beanbag wins a point or a penny. Once the round is completed, another player demonstrates a new way of traveling to the finish line and a new way to carry the beanbag with the other players following suit. Continue playing until one player has earned ten points or ten pennies.

EXAMPLE: Dad designates a start line and finish line and creates a scoring sheet on paper to track how many points each player earns. Rachel takes her turn first. She balances the beanbag on her forearm while hopping on one foot. She drops the beanbag before she reaches the finish line, so she does not earn a point. Jennifer and Louise each take their turns, and only Louise makes it to the finish line without dropping her beanbag, so she earns a point. Dad records the point on the scoring sheet.

In the next round, Louise is first, and she crawls on the floor while balancing the beanbag on her back. She makes it to the finish line without dropping the bag, so she earns a point. Jennifer and Rachel follow Louise and both earn points.

Now it is Jennifer's turn. She decides to skip to the finish line while balancing the beanbag on her head. She makes it successfully and earns a point. Rachel and Louise try it, but only Rachel makes it to the finish line without dropping the beanbag.

They continue to play until one player earns ten points.

HINTS AND VARIATIONS

- 💡 Start with simple ways to travel to the finish line, like walking or jogging.
- 💡 Each method of travel to the finish line may be used only once in each game.
- 💡 Make this a noncompetitive game by eliminating the tokens or rewards for each successful trip to the finish line.
- 💡 If players earn pennies for each successful trip to the finish line, have them carry their pennies while traveling to the finish line on subsequent turns.

SKILLS DEVELOPED: *Beanbag Balance* is a physical game that challenges players to carefully observe other players and translate their observations into actions. Players must use their coordination and gross motor skills to balance the beanbag on their body. When it's their turn to create a new way of traveling with the beanbag, players use their imaginations to generate a creative idea. The competitive nature of this game adds to the fun.

PICKUP STICKS

PURPOSE: To exercise observation skills and fine motor skills by trying to pick up a toothpick without disrupting any others.

MATERIALS NEEDED: At least 20 toothpicks or other sticks, small box with lid

NUMBER OF PLAYERS: 2 or more

HOW TO PLAY: Place the toothpicks in the box and put the lid on. Shake the box, remove the lid, and dump out the toothpicks onto a table or flat surface. Players take turns removing one toothpick without disturbing any other toothpicks. If a player does this successfully, she keeps that toothpick. If another toothpick moves in the process, the player must return the toothpick he was trying to remove back to the pile. Once all toothpicks have been removed, players add up the number of toothpicks they have earned.

EXAMPLE: Mom, Tracy, and Michael place thirty toothpicks in a shoebox. Michael shakes the box and Tracy pours the toothpicks onto a table. Michael goes first. He removes a toothpick that is not touching any others, so he does not disturb any other toothpicks. He keeps the toothpick. Tracy successfully removes a toothpick. Mom does the same. On Michael's second turn, he accidentally bumps another toothpick while trying to remove one, so he does not keep the toothpick.

Play continues until all toothpicks have been removed. Then all players count the number of toothpicks in their piles.

HINTS AND VARIATIONS

- 💡 You may play with sticks that are longer than toothpicks, such as bamboo skewers.
- 💡 Vary the starting number of toothpicks depending on the number and skill of the players.
- 💡 When playing for the first time, point out the best toothpicks to target for pickup on any given turn and explain why.
- 💡 Using colored toothpicks helps players understand spatial relationships among the toothpicks in the pile.
- 💡 For advanced players using colored sticks, assign two points to the red sticks and one point to all other colors. When the sticks are counted at the end, each red stick counts for twice as much as any other stick.

SKILLS DEVELOPED: In *Pickup Sticks,* players first examine the pile of toothpicks to select the toothpick with the best potential to be picked up. This involves visual observation and spatial ability, as players must understand how the pile of individual toothpicks fits together as a whole and what physical relationship each toothpick has to the others.

Next, players practice their fine motor skills by trying to pick up a toothpick without bumping any others. At the end of the game, children use their counting skills to determine which player has the most toothpicks.

TOOTHPICK ONE, TWO, THREE

PURPOSE: To use critical thinking in determining how many toothpicks to pick up at a time in order to win the game.

MATERIALS NEEDED: At least 15 toothpicks or other sticks

NUMBER OF PLAYERS: 2 or more

HOW TO PLAY: Lay fifteen toothpicks on a table. The first player takes one, two, or three toothpicks from the pile. The next player does the same. Continue rotating turns, with players taking one, two, or three toothpicks on each turn. The player who picks up the last toothpick loses the game.

EXAMPLE: Grandpa lays fifteen toothpicks on the table. Stephen goes first. He picks up two from the pile, leaving thirteen. Grandpa selects one, leaving twelve. Stephen picks up three, leaving nine. Grandpa picks up one. Stephen takes two. Grandpa picks up one. Stephen chooses one. Grandpa picks up three toothpicks. Stephen is left with the last toothpick.

HINTS AND VARIATIONS

- 💡 You may want to start with more than fifteen toothpicks.
- 💡 Don't rush the players. Give them plenty of time to think about how many toothpicks to pick up.

SKILLS DEVELOPED: *Toothpick One, Two, Three* involves strategic thinking, planning, and addition and subtraction skills for sophisticated players. For most preschoolers, however, this will initially be a game of chance. Nevertheless, it exercises problem-solving and visual observation. Because it can be played on many different levels, this game is likely to entertain children for years.

RATTLESNAKE

PURPOSE: To use listening skills to identify an object inside a container.

MATERIALS NEEDED: Empty film canister; 10 different objects that will each fit inside the film canister (you will need two of each object, making 20); bag

NUMBER OF PLAYERS: 2 or more

HOW TO PLAY: Gather ten small objects that will fit inside the empty film canister, such as dried pasta, a cotton ball, rice, a paper clip, a doll's shoe, a coin, a pea, a pen cap, and a piece of candy. Two of each object are needed for the game. The first set of objects is for display; arrange them on a table or a tray. Put the second set inside a bag. Objects will be drawn from this second set for placing inside the film canister.

Secretly select one object from the bag and place it inside the canister. Snap on the cover. Each player may hold the canister and shake it but may not open it. Players compare the sound made by the object in the canister with all the objects on the display tray and try to guess which of those objects is inside the canister.

Players take turns guessing until one of the players correctly identifies the object in the canister. The adult discreetly takes the object and replaces it with another one, and the guessing begins all over again. In the second round, the second player goes first.

EXAMPLE: Dad collects ten pairs of small objects two pennies, two nickels, two pencil erasers, two seashells, two rolls of film, two mints, two pretzels, two grapes, two keys, and two acorns—and lays one set out on a tray. He places one set inside a bag and closes it. In the first round, Dad takes the pencil eraser out of the bag and puts it into the film canister. He hands the film canister to Alyssa, James, and Faith. They each shake it and look at the objects on the tray to try to guess what is inside.

Alyssa guesses first, "Is it a grape?" That answer is incorrect. "Is it a pencil eraser?" asks James. That is the correct answer.

Dad replaces the eraser with a seashell. All three kids shake the canister. In this round, it is James's turn to guess first: "Is it a penny?" That answer is incorrect, so Faith guesses next. "Is it an acorn?" That answer is also incorrect. Alyssa guesses seashell and the round ends. They continue playing until all objects have been guessed.

HINTS AND VARIATIONS
- 💡 Do not use film canisters that are sheer or see-through.
- 💡 To make this game more challenging, use only one set of objects—the set in the film canister. Do not display any objects for players to choose from.

- ☼ Increasing the number of selections increases the complexity. Try playing with fifteen or twenty objects. You may even place fifteen or twenty objects on the display tray but use only ten or twelve of these in the film canister. This wider selection requires more thought from the players.

- ☼ Another way to make this game more challenging is to include similar objects on the display tray, such as a nickel and a penny, or two different kinds of pasta.

- ☼ Instead of rotating the first guess in each round, allow the correct guesser from the previous round to guess in the next round.

- ☼ To make this game more competitive, award points or even the objects themselves for every correct guess. At the end of the game, players count up their objects to see who has acquired the most.

SKILLS DEVELOPED: *Rattlesnake* can be played as a competitive or noncompetitive game. In the competitive version, players get the additional skill-building exercise of counting and comparing scores to determine a winner. In both versions, however, the main thought process relied on is auditory observation skills. Players must listen critically to the sound of the object shaking in the film canister to try to guess what it is. Offering options on a tray helps them narrow the field, but players must focus on collecting information through their ears. As they listen to the sound of the object, they consider each object on the tray and ask themselves what kind of sound that object would be expected to make, and then compare that expectation with the sound they hear. This thought process translates the auditory information into a guess.

EGG CARTON RACE

PURPOSE: To exercise categorizing skills by sorting objects into sections of an egg carton.

MATERIALS NEEDED: Empty egg cartons (one for each player); small bowls (one for each player); mixed crackers, mixed nuts, M&Ms, mixed beans, or Froot Loops cereal

NUMBER OF PLAYERS: 2 or more

HOW TO PLAY: Each player receives an empty egg carton and a bowl of objects to sort, such as mixed crackers, mixed nuts, Froot Loops cereal, or M&Ms. Players race to sort their objects by color, size, or shape into the individual egg carton cups.

EXAMPLE: Mom gives Amy and Allie each a bowl of Froot Loops and an empty egg carton. When Mom says "Go!" the girls race each other to sort their Froot Loops into the egg carton cups, placing one color in each cup. They sort for several minutes. Allie is the first to finish.

HINTS AND VARIATIONS

- 💡 The noncompetitive version of this game has players sorting objects at a leisurely pace, not racing against each other.
- 💡 There should be at least three or four different types of the object for sorting (i.e., three or four colors of cereal loops, or three or four different types of crackers).

SKILLS DEVELOPED: This simple game focuses on the categorizing thought process. It involves visual observation, as players must look at each object to determine in which egg carton cup it belongs. It also involves manual dexterity and fine motor skills, as players are sorting small objects.

HOLIDAY BINGO

PURPOSE: To use auditory and visual observation skills to mark squares on a bingo card.

MATERIALS NEEDED: Markers, heavyweight paper or cardboard, stickers related to a central theme, bowl, pennies

NUMBER OF PLAYERS: 2 or more

HOW TO PLAY: In the first phase of this game, have players create their own bingo cards. Draw a grid for each player on heavyweight paper or cardboard. The players place a sticker in each square on the grid. The stickers should have a central theme, such as an upcoming holiday, birthdays, or a special interest of the players. Place one copy of each sticker in a bowl.

In the second phase, give each player several pennies. Draw a sticker out of the bowl and call it out. Players search for this sticker on their bingo cards. If they have it, they place a penny on the sticker. Draw another sticker out of the bowl and repeat. Once a player creates a consecutive line of pennies in every square across, down, or diagonally on his card, he calls out "Bingo!" and wins the game.

EXAMPLE: A week before Jenna's birthday, Mom, Jenna, Michael, and Lisa create birthday bingo cards. They use a set of birthday stickers that show balloons, party hats, presents, noisemakers, a banner, and confetti. Mom puts one of each sticker into a bowl. She hands out a pile of pennies to each player and begins pulling stickers from the bowl. The first sticker she calls out is the balloon sticker. Jenna and Michael each have two balloon squares on their card, and Lisa has one. The players place pennies on all the balloon squares. Next

Mom takes out a party hat sticker. Michael has three party hat squares, Lisa has two, and Jenna has none. The players place pennies on these squares. Play continues in this manner.

Eventually Michael gets a consecutive row of pennies across the middle of his card. He says "Bingo!" and is the winner. In the next game, Michael gets to take the stickers out of the bowl and call them out.

HINTS AND VARIATIONS

-ᶖ- Use stickers with themes such as Halloween, birthday parties, winter, flowers, bugs, the beach, and Independence Day.

-ᶖ- Vary the size of the bingo card based on the age and skill level of the players. First-time players may create a card that's three squares by three squares, while advanced players may create a card that's five squares by five squares. The bigger the card, the longer the game.

-ᶖ- New players will need a detailed explanation of the goal of the game and a demonstration of a consecutive row or column of pennies.

-ᶖ- Be sure players understand that when they create their bingo card, they must place one sticker inside each square and nowhere else on the card.

SKILLS DEVELOPED: The two distinct phases of *Holiday Bingo* stimulate a wide variety of thinking processes. In creating the bingo cards, players exercise fine motor skills and visual observation skills to select and place stickers on the grid. In playing the game, players must rely on auditory observation skills to gather information about which sticker to cover with a penny. Then they shift gears to visual observation to find that sticker and place a penny on it. Finally, they use problem-solving skills to check their card and determine whether they have a consecutive row or column of pennies.

INVENTORY

PURPOSE: To use counting and categorizing skills to take inventory of household items and graph the results.

MATERIALS NEEDED: Plain paper, graph paper, crayons or markers, scissors, bowl or large jar

NUMBER OF PLAYERS: 1 or more

HOW TO PLAY: Players draw pictures of several household and clothing items that are plentiful around their house, such as socks, sweaters, spoons, and keys. Each picture is cut out and placed into a bowl for that player. Once a day, a different picture is taken out of that player's bowl. The player must then locate and count all these objects in the house.

When they are all counted, help the player create and fill in a single bar on a bar graph. If graph paper is not available, draw blocks on plain paper. Each day, the player adds another bar to the bar graph. The object counted is written underneath each bar. Over time, players can compare the inventory of the items to one another.

EXAMPLE: Laura and Jillian draw several pictures of items around the house. Laura draws a plate, a ball, a pencil, a telephone, a shoe, a chair, a toothbrush, and a fork. Jillian draws a mug, a stuffed animal, a key, a table, a pillow, a jacket, and a dress. Laura and Jillian cut out their pictures and place them in separate bowls. Mom makes graph paper for each player, and the girls write their names at the top of their pages.

Laura pulls a picture of a shoe out of her bowl. Mom suggests she exclude adult shoes and count only children's shoes. Laura goes around the house finding and counting shoes. She loses count a couple of times and has to start over. Mom shows her how to keep count by drawing a line on a piece of paper for every shoe that she finds. Laura finds twelve pairs of shoes. Meanwhile, Jillian takes a picture of a key out of her bowl. She asks Mom for the key chains and counts sixteen keys.

The girls sit down to fill in their graphs with Mom's help. The next day, they play again, adding another bar to the graph.

HINTS AND VARIATIONS

- Make sure that when children select household items to count, they don't select items that are *too* plentiful, such as books (if you have hundreds). If they do select something with a very high count, limit their inventory taking to the books on one bookshelf or in one room.
- It is not necessary to spread this game over several days or to play every day. Players may enjoy taking inventory of three or four items on the first day, and then skip a few days before playing again.
- If players are having trouble thinking of household items to draw pictures of, suggest articles of clothing.
- Skip the drawing phase and place words in a bowl or jar and draw a word out each day instead of a picture.
- Players can continue to draw pictures and add them to the bowl of drawings after the initial start of the game.
- Players are likely to lose count as they walk around taking inventory. Show them how to draw a line on piece of paper to represent every object they find, and count the lines when they are done.

SKILLS DEVELOPED: Players use their imagination to generate ideas for household items to draw. Drawing representational pictures for these items may be difficult for many players. Offer suggestions and be encouraging, and let the players take their time with the drawings. It's not important for others to be able to recognize the object they've drawn. With practice, their drawings will become more representational, and they will become more comfortable drawing a wide variety of objects.

inventory-taking portion of this game, visual observation skills are sharpened and the concept of representation is explored. If players keep count of objects with lines on a piece of paper, that's a first lesson in representation. The second lesson comes when the bar charts are created, and players realize that the bar represents the number of objects they've counted. Take time to review the bar results after several items have been charted. Discuss the relationship between the different bars by asking questions about which items received the highest count, the lowest, and so on, to help players understand the meaning of the bars.

LETTER MATCH

PURPOSE: To sharpen visual observation skills by searching for matching letters, and to exercise imagination and language skills by generating words that have particular sounds.

MATERIALS NEEDED: Two sets of alphabet letters (magnetic letters, tub letters, puzzle letters, or block letters); bowl

NUMBER OF PLAYERS: 1 or more

HOW TO PLAY: Place one set of alphabet letters in a bowl and spread out the other set on a flat surface. Each player selects one letter from the bowl and searches the other set of letters to find the matching letter. Once all players have found their matching letters, the first player must name three words that begin with her letter. The next player must name three words that begin with his letter. Play continues until all letters have been selected.

EXAMPLE: Elizabeth draws an M and Katie takes a Z from the bowl. Each player finds the matching letter from the set of letters laid out on the table. Then Elizabeth names three words that begin with M: *monkey, melon,* and *melt.* Next Katie names three words that begin with Z: *zebra, zipper,* and *zoom.*

Each player draws another letter. Elizabeth gets a Y and Katie gets an E. They find the matching letters, and each player names three words that begin with those letters. They continue playing until the bowl is empty.

HINTS AND VARIATIONS

- To simplify this game, play with one set of letters instead of two, and skip the matching exercise.
- Give clues to children who are having trouble thinking of words.
- You may make an exception for the letter X, and require only one or two words beginning with that letter.
- For children who have mastered beginning letters, a more challenging version of this game is to have players generate words that *end* instead of *start* with the chosen letter.
- For players learning how to read and write, ask that they write one word for each letter sound on a piece of paper, with your help if necessary.
- Instead of playing until the letters run out, players may return the letters to the bowl and table after they're picked. If they're picked again, the player who picks the letter the second time can't repeat the same words.
- Make this game competitive by awarding one point for every word identified that begins with the selected letter, and two points for every word identified that ends with the selected letter. You may also offer a bonus point for long words, that is, words with three or more syllables.

SKILLS DEVELOPED: Visual observation is the first skill that *Letter Match* focuses on, because children must carefully examine the letters laid out on the table to find the one that matches the letter they draw out of the bowl. Language and expression is the second skill, because children must draw on their knowledge of words and sounds to generate three words that begin with the letter they've drawn. Imagination is also a factor, as children must draw upon their imagination to identify words with the right sounds.

TRACING GAME

PURPOSE: To stimulate motor skills by tracing household objects, and to use spatial abilities to solve tracing puzzles created by other players.

MATERIALS NEEDED: Variety of small household objects; paper; markers, crayons, or pencils

NUMBER OF PLAYERS: 2 or more

HOW TO PLAY: Players collect several household objects or toys and trace their outlines onto paper. The objects should be small enough so that five will fit on one sheet of paper. When all players have created at least five outlines, they switch papers with each other. All the objects are placed in the center of the table. The players race to match up the objects with their outlines by placing the correct object on top of each outline. The first player to complete the puzzle wins the round.

EXAMPLE: Robert, Henry, and Jessica each gather five household items to trace. Robert traces a pencil, a button, a penny, a piece of candy, and a baby shoe. Henry traces an envelope, a spoon, a quarter, a nickel, and a paper clip. Jessica traces a key, a small book, a rabbit figurine, a doll's shoe, and a staple.

Then the players switch papers, and all the objects are placed in a pile in the center of the table. They race each other to find the objects that match up to the outlines on their papers. Henry is the first to lay all five objects down on the page that Jessica had created.

HINTS AND VARIATIONS

-ᛘ- If some players finish tracing objects before others, have them color in the outlines that they've created.

-ᛘ- To make this game more challenging, increase the number of objects that players are drawing on their papers from five to eight or ten.

-ᛘ- It is not necessary for this game to be competitive. Players can match up objects with outlines at a leisurely pace.

-ᛘ- If you would like to limit the objects that players trace, gather fifteen or twenty objects and place them in a basket before the game begins. Let the children select objects out of this basket.

SKILLS DEVELOPED: First, players must use their imagination to generate ideas for objects to trace. Their imagination must be tempered by reality, because objects must be small enough to fit five or more on one page. Second, players use their fine motor skills to hold the object down with one hand while tracing it with the other hand. Third, after players switch papers, they use their spatial abilities and visual observation skills to determine which objects fit in which outlines.

PHOTO SAFARI

PURPOSE: To exercise visual observation and prereading skills in matching pictures with words.

MATERIALS NEEDED: Camera and film, paper, scissors, pen or marker

NUMBER OF PLAYERS: 1 or more

HOW TO PLAY: Take a photo safari through your neighborhood with your children. Together, take photos of familiar objects such as a fire hydrant, a house, a sign, a dog, and a fence. After the film is developed, create small cards with a word on each one that identifies the subject of each photo. Lay the photos and the word cards out on a table. Players take turns selecting a photo and trying to find the matching word.

EXAMPLE: Molly and her father walk through the neighborhood and take photos of a mailbox, a fence, a swing set, Whiskers the cat, a UPS truck, a neighbor's car, a number on a house, a lamp, a street sign, a flowering bush, and a tree. After the pictures are developed, Molly and Dad make cards with a one-word description of each photo. The cards and the photos are laid out on a table. One at a time, Molly selects a photo and searches for the matching card. Dad gives her a few hints. Once she finds the match, Molly places the pair in a pile. She continues until she finds a match for each picture.

HINTS AND VARIATIONS

- To make this game challenging and interesting, include several photos in the game—at least eight or ten, and as many as twenty.
- Include photos of people as well as objects.
- Prereaders will initially rely on the first letter of a word to find matches. To encourage them to look at an entire word, make sure a few words begin with the same letter.

🔆 Your child can help create the word cards by cutting the paper or by writing letters dictated by you.

🔆 Consider writing in lowercase letters on the word cards.

🔆 If your preschool child is already reading, make this game more challenging by using less obvious words or phrases to describe each photo.

SKILLS DEVELOPED: Although this game is similar in format to typical reading exercises, the fact that it is personalized for your children by using photos of their own environment makes it more meaningful and fun. Involving your children in the setup by taking them on the Photo Safari is a great way to build interest.

This game is ideal for a child who can easily identify sounds by letter but is not yet reading on his own. It builds beginning reading skills by stimulating visual observation and language skills. After playing a few times, your child may begin to memorize the word that corresponds with each photo.

WRAP IT UP

PURPOSE: To use visual observation and matching skills to find the other half of a piece of wrapping paper or fabric.

MATERIALS NEEDED: Scraps of wrapping paper and/or fabric, in at least eight different patterns; scissors; bag or bowl

NUMBER OF PLAYERS: 1 or more

HOW TO PLAY: Gather scraps of wrapping paper and/or fabric. With your children, cut each scrap into two pieces. Hide one half of each scrap in somewhat obvious hiding spots throughout one room or a few rooms. Place the other halves in a bag or bowl. Players take turns reaching into the bag for a scrap, and then searching for its mate. Once a player finds a mate, he returns to the bag to draw a new scrap. Play continues until all scraps have been matched.

EXAMPLE: Mom gathers several fabric scraps, and Owen and Lily help cut each one in half. While the children wait upstairs, Mom hides one half of each scrap throughout the living room and dining room and places the other half of each scrap in a shopping bag. Mom calls the children downstairs and lets each one pull a scrap out of the bag.

Owen pulls out a scrap of solid red fabric, and Lily takes out a scrap of yellow flowered fabric. They both search for the matching half. Owen finds his first and returns both halves to Mom. Then he pulls another scrap from the bag. When Lily finds hers, she does the same. Mom keeps separate piles for Owen's and Lily's matches.

When all the scraps have been matched, Owen and Lily count the pieces of fabric in their piles. Owen has sixteen and Lily has eighteen.

HINTS AND VARIATIONS

- 🔅 Gather enough scraps so that on average each child searches for six to twelve matches.
- 🔅 Starting scraps should measure at least 2 inches by 4 inches so that they will measure two by two when cut. Larger scraps will work, too.
- 🔅 Make sure kids understand that they cannot pick up scraps that do not match the one they hold in their hand.
- 🔅 Finding the matching scraps gets easier as the game progresses because children have probably seen many of the hidden scraps as they searched for a particular pattern in earlier rounds.
- 🔅 This game may be made competitive by keeping piles of found matches for each child, and then having the children count the scraps in their piles at the end of the game.

- ☀ If there are two or more players, let the winner of each game hide the scraps in the next game.
- ☀ This game can be played with children of varying ages.

SKILLS DEVELOPED: In the preparation phase, children stimulate their fine motor skills when they help cut the scraps in half. When they search for matches, they exercise both their visual observation skills and their problem-solving skills, as they compare each scrap to the scrap in their hand to determine whether they match.

If the competitive version of this game is played and children count the number of scraps they find, counting skills are called into play. Finally, if children are given the opportunity to hide the scraps, they must use their imagination to think of creative hiding spots.

PHOTO SORT

PURPOSE: To use visual observation and sorting skills to organize photos chronologically.

MATERIALS NEEDED: Several photos of each player at different ages

NUMBER OF PLAYERS: 1 or more

HOW TO PLAY: Gather several different photos of each player, starting from baby photos and going through the child's current age. Lay the photos of one child out of sequence on a table. The first player finds the photo of the child at the youngest age. He takes the photo and puts it aside. The next player selects the next youngest photo and lays it next to the first. Play continues, with each player selecting the next chronological photo. If a selection is incorrect, the player must put it back and the next player takes his turn.

Once the chronologically correct line of photos has been created, walk through the photos as a group and discuss the age of the child in each one. Then play again using pictures of another player.

EXAMPLE: Dad collects several photos of Michaela and Richard. He lays the photos of Michaela out of sequence on a table. Michaela selects a baby photo and starts a line. Dad confirms it is the youngest photo. Then Richard selects another photo. Dad tells him there is a younger photo than that one. Richard returns the photo, and Michaela takes her turn next.

The players continue taking turns selecting photos and laying each selection down. When the chronological line of photos has been created, Dad lays out photos of Richard, and the players follow the same process.

HINTS AND VARIATIONS

- Start with five to twelve photos of each player.
- If you remove the photos from a photo album, mark the empty spots in the photo album with small notes so you can easily return the photos to their respective locations when the game is over.
- Make this game more challenging by creating small cards with ages written on each one. After creating the chronological line of photos, players take turns selecting an age card and placing the correct one under each photo.
- To make this game competitive, award a token or a penny for each photo placed correctly in line. At the end, players count their pennies to determine who has the most.

SKILLS DEVELOPED: Kids love to look at photos of themselves as babies. This game takes advantage of that natural interest and encourages children to think about sequence. Putting the photos in chronological order helps children develop the problem-solving skill for sequencing. Children must also rely on visual observation to critically examine each photo to determine where it fits in the line of photos.

PLACEWARES

PURPOSE: To exercise visual observation and sorting skills in setting the table.

MATERIALS NEEDED: Several different patterns of paper plates, napkins, and cups from past birthday parties and holiday occasions; box; bowl

NUMBER OF PLAYERS: 1 or more

HOW TO PLAY: Save paper plates, napkins, and cups from past birthday and holiday occasions in a box. When it's time for a meal, remove one napkin or plate from each pattern and place it in a bowl. Each player draws one item out of the bowl and finds the accompanying pieces in the box to make one place setting at the table. Players may go back for a second round to set places for the adults, too. At the end of the game, each place at the table will have a unique set of matching plate, napkin, and cup.

EXAMPLE: In a box, Mom had saved the paper goods from Terry's first birthday, Alex's dinosaur party, Jason's Winnie-the-Pooh party, Terry's Little Mermaid party, a Christmas party, Mitchell's christening, and a fortieth birthday party for Dad. At lunchtime one day, she places one napkin from each party in a bowl. Each player selects a napkin out of the bowl and then searches through the box to find a matching plate, cup, and fork. Each player then sets one place at the table using her or his selected pattern. Then they each draw another napkin out of the bowl, go back to the box, find the matching pattern, and set another place at the table. At the end, the table is set with six unique place settings.

HINTS AND VARIATIONS

- Purchase new paper goods if you wish, but you may prefer to save leftovers from parties and celebrations.
- On a different night, rather than set matching place settings, challenge players to set mixed-up place settings, with each paper good from a different celebration.

SKILLS DEVELOPED: Rummaging through a box of old paper goods is likely to bring back happy memories for your children. This game stimulates sorting, matching skills, and visual observation skills. It also makes the process of setting the table a fun game.

RED DAY

PURPOSE: To use visual observation and imagination to determine how to incorporate a color into a particular day.

MATERIALS NEEDED: Scissors, paper, markers or crayons, bowl or jar, paper and pencil

NUMBER OF PLAYERS: 1 or more

HOW TO PLAY: Cut the paper into five or more small pieces. Ask the players to scribble a unique color on each piece of paper, then label the color with a word. Put the papers in a bowl.

Draw one color out of the jar. This will be tomorrow's color of the day. If it's red, then tomorrow will be Red Day. Brainstorm ways to incorporate this color into your day tomorrow. For example, players may wear red clothes, eat red foods at dinner, write with a red pencil, and play with red toys. Use as many of these ideas as you can to reinforce the color theme for that day.

On the color day, encourage children to count every red item they use, wear, or eat while at home. Give them paper and a pencil and have them draw a line for each red item. At the end of the day, they can count their lines.

EXAMPLE: Angie and Joey create slips of paper for red, yellow, purple, orange, green, and blue. Mom places them in a jar, and Joey pulls out the green one. The next day will be Green Day. The family brainstorms about ways to incorporate the color green into their day.

That night, Angie sleeps with a green blanket and Joey brings a stuffed green dinosaur to bed. When they wake up, they use green toothpaste and green towels. The kids keep track of all the green things they use by making a line on a piece of paper for each one. For breakfast, Mom adds green food coloring to their scrambled eggs. Angie and Joey dress in green clothes and put green pencils in their backpacks. For lunch, Mom packs green grapes, celery, cucumber slices, and a sandwich with lettuce. When the kids return from school, they play catch with a green ball, watch a video that came in a green case, and play with green stuffed animals. For dinner, Mom and Dad serve green salad and spinach fettuccini with broccoli florets and peas. For dessert, they eat mint chocolate chip ice cream. After dinner they draw green pictures.

That evening, Angie and Joey count the number of lines they have made on their papers. Joey has thirty-seven and Angie has twenty-eight.

HINTS AND VARIATIONS

- Consider using food coloring to add an unusual color to foods you are cooking, such as scrambled eggs.
- When you brainstorm about how to incorporate the colors into the day, create a list.
- It may be wise to limit this game to the time that children are at home with you.

SKILLS DEVELOPED: *Red Day* helps children look at everyday tasks and activities in a whole new way. Eating green eggs, for example, is more fun than eating yellow eggs. Children stimulate their imaginations by thinking about all the ways they can incorporate a color into their day. They also use counting skills when they tally up the number of colored objects that they ate, touched, or used throughout the day.

BLIND SHAPES

PURPOSE: To identify shapes through the sense of touch.

MATERIALS NEEDED: Poster board or cardboard, scissors, large sock, pen or pencil, paper, bowl or jar

NUMBER OF PLAYERS: 1 or more

HOW TO PLAY: Cut poster board into shapes such as a circle, star, triangle, and square. Stuff the shapes into a large sock. Write the name of each shape on a small piece of paper and put the pieces of paper into a bowl or jar. One at a time, players reach into the jar and select a shape. They must reach into the sock to find that shape without looking. If they pull out the incorrect shape, it is returned to the sock and the next player tries to find the correct shape. If they pull out the correct shape, they keep it in their pile.

Play continues until all shapes have been correctly pulled out. Then players count the number of shapes in their winning piles.

EXAMPLE: Caroline and William gathered magnet shapes of a moon, star, circle, square, rectangle, diamond, triangle, hexagon, octagon, and heart. Then they help Mom cut out slips of paper. Mom writes the name of a shape on each piece of paper and puts these words in a jar. The shapes are stuffed inside a large sock.

Caroline goes first. She draws the word *triangle* out of the jar. She then reaches into the sock, feels around, and pulls out a star. Since this is incorrect, she returns it to the sock, and William takes his turn. He pulls the triangle out of the sock and keeps it in his winning pile. Caroline reaches into the jar and pulls out the word *circle*. She sticks her hand into the sock and successfully pulls out the circle. Play continues until all the shapes have been correctly removed from the sock.

The players count the number of shapes they have each won. Caroline has six and William has four.

HINTS AND VARIATIONS

- Try to include at least seven or eight shapes in the sock, or more if you have more than three players.
- Use small plastic or wooden shapes from a game or puzzle instead of cutting out the shapes.
- Let the players take their time feeling around inside the sock.
- If you have shapes that are too big to fit into a sock, use a larger container, such as a bowl with a towel over it, or an empty box.
- For advanced players, include more complex shapes such as hexagon, octagon, parallelogram, and trapezoid.
- It isn't necessary for this game to be competitive. Players may simply take turns without keeping a pile of their winning shapes.

SKILLS DEVELOPED: *Blind Shapes* gives players the opportunity to focus on gathering information from just one isolated sense: their sense of touch. Players should not be allowed to gather any other clues by looking at the shapes in the sock. If the competitive version of this game is played, children use problem-solving skills to count the number of items they correctly identified throughout the game.

LETTER DOUGH

PURPOSE: To use artistic expression and fine motor skills while creating letters out of clay and identifying word sounds.

MATERIALS NEEDED: Alphabet letters, box or bowl, Play-Doh or similar type of children's clay

NUMBER OF PLAYERS: 1 or more

HOW TO PLAY: Place the alphabet letters into a box. Each player closes her eyes and selects one letter from the box. The player is challenged to think of three words that begin with that letter. While she is thinking, she takes a piece of clay and shapes it into her letter. She then names three words. The player reaches for another letter and plays again. Continue playing several rounds. If there are several players, you may create an entire clay alphabet.

EXAMPLE: Kate and David put their magnetic alphabet letters into a bowl. Kate pulls out the first letter, a Z. As she thinks of three words beginning with that letter, she makes the letter Z out of Play-Doh. By the time she forms the letter, she has identified three words: *zebra, zipper,* and *zoo.* At the same time, David picks the letter C. He creates a C out of Play-Doh and says the words *cry, cook,* and *cockatoo.* Kate and David continue playing until all the letters have been drawn from the bowl.

HINTS AND VARIATIONS

- This game is best played at a leisurely pace. It should not be a race.
- First-time players may need a demonstration of how to roll the clay into snake shapes and bend them to form letters.
- When playing with a group that includes older children, challenge those players to think of three words that *end* with the selected letter rather than begin with it.
- Rather than draw letters out of a bowl, each player may work to spell his first name in clay.
- Children who are learning their lowercase letters may be challenged to create a lowercase letter out of clay rather than uppercase.

SKILLS DEVELOPED: *Letter Dough* gives players the opportunity to focus on one letter of the alphabet while completing two activities: working with their hands to form it and thinking about its sound. As a result, this game stimulates both fine motor skills and language skills.

BE A PENCIL

PURPOSE: To cultivate gross motor skills and physical artistic expression to imitate an inanimate object.

MATERIALS NEEDED: Scissors, paper, pencil, bowl

NUMBER OF PLAYERS: 2 or more

HOW TO PLAY: As a group, cut several small pieces of paper. On each slip of paper, write the name and draw a picture of an inanimate object. Place the papers in a bowl. Players take turns drawing a piece of paper out of the bowl (they may need help to decipher the word). They then twist their bodies to imitate the object on the paper, and the other players try to guess what the object is. The actor may give clues if players are having a difficult time guessing the object. The player who correctly guesses the object is the next to pick a paper out of the bowl and act out that object.

EXAMPLE: Audrey draws the word *Jell-O* out of the bowl. To act like Jell-O, she wiggles her body. The other players make several guesses, and finally Lauren guesses Jell-O. Next Lauren draws the word *tree*. She stands very straight and holds her arms up in the air, swaying them slowly from side to side as she wiggles her fingers. After several guesses, Beth says "Tree." Next, Beth picks the word *train*. She bends her legs and moves her arms in a chugging motion. When Lauren can't make a guess, Beth starts saying "Choo-choo." Audrey guesses train. The children continue playing several rounds.

HINTS AND VARIATIONS

- 💡 Begin by explaining to players what an inanimate object is.
- 💡 Suggestions for inanimate objects include: a popping toaster, a ringing telephone, a bed, an opening and closing refrigerator, an elevator, a floppy stuffed animal, a tree blowing in the wind, falling rain, a moving car, popping popcorn, hair blowing in the wind, an opening and closing door, a standing house, a swinging swing, wiggling Jell-O, and, of course, a stiff, straight pencil.
- 💡 You may read all the options in the bowl to the players before beginning, so the players have some clue as to what the actor may be portraying.
- 💡 Players are encouraged to begin acting out their object silently. After some time, if the other players are having difficulty guessing

it, they can add sound effects. If that doesn't help, they can give verbal clues.

- A more challenging version of this game has players thinking of inanimate objects on their own, without pulling words out of a bowl.

SKILLS DEVELOPED: This challenging game requires creativity and imagination. The act of using one's body to effectively portray an inanimate object is a form of artistic expression. Critical thinking is necessary to think about how that object would act. For example, how would you move your body to resemble Jell-O or an elevator? The players who are guessing also have a difficult task. They must also use critical thinking to translate the actor's movements into an inanimate object.

RAINBOW SNACK

PURPOSE: To exercise visual observation skills, categorizing abilities, counting skills, and manual dexterity.

MATERIALS NEEDED: M&Ms, paper, pen or pencil

NUMBER OF PLAYERS: 1 or more

HOW TO PLAY: Give each player at least twenty M&M candies. Have each player group his candies into piles of the same color. Ask them to count the number of M&Ms in each pile. Write the totals on small slips of paper placed in front of each pile.

The players determine which pile has the greatest number of M&Ms. The owner of that pile eats those candies. The players then determine which of the remaining piles has the largest number of M&Ms. The owner of that pile eats those M&Ms. If there is a tie between two or more players' piles, they can be eaten simultaneously. If there is a tie between a player's own piles, the player may choose to eat either pile. Continue until all the M&Ms are gone.

EXAMPLE: Sam, Nolan, and Mom each receive twenty-two M&Ms and sort them into five lines, one for each color. As they count their M&Ms, the counts are written on slips of paper in front of each pile.

SAM'S M&MS	NOLAN'S M&MS	MOM'S M&MS
8 red	3 red	5 red
6 brown	7 brown	9 brown
4 green	5 green	2 green
2 yellow	3 yellow	6 yellow
2 blue	4 blue	0 blue

The trio concludes that Mom's pile of nine brown M&Ms is the largest, so she eats that pile. Next, Sam's pile of eight red M&Ms is the next largest, and he eats that pile. Nolan eats his pile of seven brown M&Ms. Sam and Mom tie with six M&Ms each, so both of them eat those piles. The group continues until all the candies are gone.

HINTS AND VARIATIONS

- Players should lay their M&Ms in straight lines to make counting and comparing easier.
- After all piles have been counted, have players donate one M&M from their largest pile to another player. For example, donate one M&M each to the oldest player, the youngest player, the player with the closest birthday, the player to her right, or the player wearing socks that match the color of that pile. Then all players recount and relabel their piles.

- 🔆 Older children may be able to write the numbers on the slips of paper themselves.
- 🔆 If there's only one player, play without the slips of paper. Line up the M&Ms and use visual observation to determine which pile is the largest.
- 🔆 You may find that children like receiving their M&Ms in a small bowl and that they use the bowl throughout the game as a categorizing tool.
- 🔆 You may use mini-M&Ms.
- 🔆 Jelly beans or mixed crackers may be substituted for M&Ms. Or, you may use a veggie mix of bite-size celery pieces, carrot pieces, cucumber pieces, and peas, or a fruit mix of grapes, blueberries, and strawberries.

SKILLS DEVELOPED: This game makes snacktime even more fun! First your child must assess the various colors of M&Ms he has received, which requires visual observation skills. Categorizing the M&Ms into distinct piles or straight lines builds problem-solving skills and manual dexterity. Comparing the size of the piles is a counting game that requires critical thinking. Your child will never look at M&Ms the same way again!

ALLIGATOR TAG

PURPOSE: To use gross motor skills while playing tag.

MATERIALS NEEDED: None

NUMBER OF PLAYERS: 2 or more

HOW TO PLAY: Have the players go to an adjacent room. Then, lie on the floor with your eyes closed. The players come into the room, sneak up to you, and try to touch you without getting caught. If you hear a player, you may open your eyes and "catch" the player, then send the player back to the adjacent room. The first player to successfully tag you wins the round.

EXAMPLE: Dad lies on the floor while Kevin, Christy, Julie, and Ben stand in the next room. One at a time, they creep toward Dad. Dad hears a sound and opens his eyes. He sends everyone back to the starting room. Again the children quietly creep forward toward Dad. Ben gets very close and almost tags Dad, but Dad hears him and opens his eyes. All the kids go back to the starting room. Finally Christy creeps up and touches Dad's toe without him hearing her. Everyone cheers for Christy, and they play again.

VARIATIONS

- This game seems to work best if an adult plays the role of alligator, but an older child may play the role.

SKILLS DEVELOPED: *Alligator Tag* is based on the traditional outdoor tag game, but it is a quiet indoor alternative that rewards children for moving slowly and silently. It should be considered a team game, in which all players work together to tag the alligator. You may see cooperation and teamwork among the children as they devise a group strategy. The primary skill developed by this game is gross motor skills, as children try to move very quietly to sneak up on the alligator.

SOCK TOSS

PURPOSE: To use gross motor skills to toss socks at a target.

MATERIALS NEEDED: Several rolled-up sock balls

NUMBER OF PLAYERS: 2 or more

HOW TO PLAY: One player is designated the target. All other players lie on the floor while the target stands facing them with arms straight down. Players take turns tossing sock balls up at the target, aiming for the hands. When a player hits a hand with a sock ball, he earns a point. When one player has accumulated five points, he becomes the target in the next round, and the previous target lies on the floor with the other players. The scores revert to zero, and the players on the floor continue to take turns tossing socks at the target.

EXAMPLE: Rebecca is assigned the role of target. She stands at one end of the family room. Joseph and Christopher lie on the floor with a pile of sock balls between them. They take turns tossing socks at Rebecca's hands. After a few minutes, Joseph hit a hand three times and Christopher hit a hand once. They continue until Joseph has five points. Then Joseph is the target, and Rebecca lies on the floor and tosses socks at him. They continue playing several rounds.

HINTS AND VARIATIONS
- Before playing this game, let the kids know what it feels like to be hit in the hand with a sock ball.
- If a player isn't comfortable with being the target, don't force her.
- This is a great game to play after doing a load of laundry. Teach children how to make sock balls, and then sort them and put them away once the game is complete.

- ☀ If the players have a hard time hitting the target, change the target to the entire arm or require just one hit before switching places.
- ☀ Advanced players can lie farther away from the target.
- ☀ Players who can't throw the socks high enough to reach the target's hand may be allowed to sit instead of lying down.
- ☀ Socks should always be thrown gently.

SKILLS DEVELOPED: *Sock Toss* is a fun physical game that helps develop gross motor skills and throwing abilities. Let children experiment with tossing from a prone position and from a standing position, so they can appreciate the difference. Explain that this game is played from a lying position to ensure that socks are tossed gently.

DRESS-UP RACE

PURPOSE: To use gross motor skills to dress quickly.

MATERIALS NEEDED: Complete outfit for each player

NUMBER OF PLAYERS: 1 or more

HOW TO PLAY: In the morning, when all players are still wearing their pajamas, select an outfit for each player to wear that day. Set the timer for five minutes and call "Go!" All players go to their rooms or dressing areas and race against the clock to be the first one dressed. Award a sticker to any player who is completely dressed before the timer sounds. Place stickers on a calendar or on a special chart that you create together. Once a player has earned five stickers, award a special prize or reward to that player.

EXAMPLE: On Monday, outfits are selected for Jonathan, Hannah, and Grace and laid out on their beds. After breakfast, Mom sets the timer for five minutes. The players go to their rooms and race against the clock to take off their pajamas and put on their selected outfits. When the timer sounds, Jonathan is completely dressed, but Hannah and Grace are not. Jonathan earns a sticker. On Tuesday, they follow the same procedure, and Hannah and Jonathan both earn stickers. On Wednesday, Jonathan and Grace win stickers. On Thursday, Grace and Hannah win. On Friday, only Grace gets a sticker. The family continues playing over the next few days. Jonathan is the first player to earn five stickers. He is rewarded with a new book. A few days later, Grace and Hannah also reach the five-sticker milestone and are rewarded with gifts.

HINTS AND VARIATIONS

- Include other activities in the race, such as brushing teeth and washing up.
- Give a head start to younger children who are slower dressers, or offer help from an adult on certain activities, such as tying shoes.
- Rewards may be gifts or privileges.
- A more competitive version of this game has players racing against each other instead of the timer. Only the first player to be dressed earns a sticker each day. At the end of a one-week or two-week period, determine which player earned the most stickers and award a prize. You may also award a second-place prize or consolation prizes for all players.

SKILLS DEVELOPED: This game transforms an everyday chore into a fun activity. It can be an exhilarating way to start the day. Be sure to even the odds with head starts so everyone has a fair shot at winning, or else it can be frustrating for slower dressers or children who are putting on more articles of clothing. The ability to dress quickly and without assistance relies on gross motor skills. Perhaps the biggest benefit of this game, however, is that it can make mornings easier for parents.

JUMPING PENNIES

PURPOSE: To use fine motor skills to create a penny triangle on paper, and to use problem-solving skills and observation skills to jump pennies.

MATERIALS NEEDED: 14 pennies; paper for each player; pen, pencil, or crayon

NUMBER OF PLAYERS: 1 or more

HOW TO PLAY: Help each player trace around a penny at the top of each child's piece of paper. Below that circle, each player creates two more circles, one on either side of the top circle. In the next row down, players create three more circles, straddling the two circles on the previous row. The next row has four pennies and the final row has five. The final picture should look like a triangle or a pyramid of pennies.

Give each player fourteen pennies to place on any fourteen of the fifteen circles on their paper. Explain that a penny may jump over an adjacent penny to land in an empty circle. After each jump, the penny that was jumped over is removed from the paper. Continue jumping pennies over pennies into empty spots until no more jumps are possible. The goal is to be left with as few pennies as possible.

EXAMPLE: Mom helps Amelia and Madeline draw their penny triangles on a piece of paper. Each player receives fourteen pennies and places them on the circles in their paper. Amelia chooses to leave the top circle empty, and Madeline leaves a circle in the middle of her triangle empty.

The children begin jumping pennies. Amelia's first move is to jump one penny from the third row up to the top empty spot and eliminate the penny in between. Madeline's first move is to jump the top penny over a penny in the second row down to the empty spot in the third row. She removes the penny in between. Amelia and Madeline continue jumping pennies. At the end, Amelia has three pennies left and Madeline has two.

HINTS AND VARIATIONS

- ☀ Make sure the players understand the concept of a jump before starting. Have them each show you a few practice jumps.
- ☀ You may create just one penny triangle for the players to share. Players take turns jumping pennies on that paper.
- ☀ First-time players are likely to need coaching for their first few games.
- ☀ Tell players that their goal is to be left with just one, two, or three pennies.

SKILLS DEVELOPED: *Jumping Pennies* requires concentration and critical thinking. Visual observation skills are stimulated as players search their penny triangle for empty spots, and problem-solving skills are stimulated as players think about the paths that their pennies may follow to jump into empty spots. After some practice, players may begin to plan ahead and think strategically about how to leave only one, two, or three pennies on their pages. Fine motor skills are also exercised as players trace the pennies and maneuver them on the paper.

ANIMAL PANTOMIMES

PURPOSE: To think creatively, solve problems, and express oneself through performance.

MATERIALS NEEDED: None

NUMBER OF PLAYERS: 2 or more

HOW TO PLAY: The first player selects an animal and then acts out the movements of that animal without making any sound. The other players try to guess which animal is being portrayed. The player who correctly identifies the animal is the next performer.

EXAMPLE: Jeanne decides to be a rabbit and begins hopping. Isabella, Beth, and Dad yell out their guesses by naming animals that hop. Beth guesses rabbit, so she goes next. Beth swims like a fish, and Isabella correctly identifies her animal. Isabella takes her turn next.

HINTS AND VARIATIONS
- 💡 If the audience needs a hint, the performer can make an animal sound as a clue.
- 💡 Examples include bear, giraffe, turtle, elephant, squirrel, alligator, mouse, dog, fish, rabbit, dinosaur, bird, cat, and frog.
- 💡 Rather than selecting their own animal, place pictures or stickers of various animals into a hat and have the players draw an animal from the hat to act out.

SKILLS DEVELOPED: Watching the other players act out animals helps sharpen observation skills. Players use their problem-solving abilities when trying to guess the animals being portrayed. When a player selects an animal to portray, she uses creative thinking and imagination. When a player acts out the animal's motions, he is using motor skills to express himself artistically.

OUTDOOR
GAMES

✲ BALLOONEY

PURPOSE: To keep a balloon off the ground using gross motor skills and hand-eye coordination.

MATERIALS NEEDED: Inflated balloon (not helium)

NUMBER OF PLAYERS: 2 or more

HOW TO PLAY: Players hit a balloon back and forth without letting it touch the ground. As a team, the players count aloud the number of hits they give the balloon. When the balloon touches the ground, the round is over. Players continue trying to beat their last score.

EXAMPLE: Dad blows up a balloon. Morgan, Chelsea, and Dad stand equidistant from one another in the backyard. Dad begins by hitting the balloon, volleyball-style, to Morgan and counting "One!" Morgan hits it to Chelsea as everyone says "Two!" Chelsea hits it to Dad and everyone shouts "Three!" When Dad hits the balloon back to Morgan, it touches the ground before Morgan can hit it. They start over and in the next round count nine consecutive hits. They continue playing several rounds. In their most successful round, they hit the balloon twenty-five times before it touches the ground.

HINTS AND VARIATIONS

- ☀ It is not necessary for the players to hit the balloon in any particular order. For example, one player may hit the balloon twice in a row.
- ☀ Counting the number of consecutive hits together out loud keeps players engaged and challenged to keep the balloon "alive."
- ☀ Demonstrate different styles of hitting the balloon based on volleyball techniques.
- ☀ Players may move from their initial starting spots.

🔆 This game works well with three players. If there are four or more players, you may consider breaking into smaller groups of two or three players. Draw a line with sidewalk chalk on the driveway and split pairs of players onto either side.

🔆 An inflated balloon may be replaced with a water balloon. Players are challenged to toss the balloon back and forth and count the number of tosses before the balloon bursts.

🔆 If there are two or more teams of players, a competitive version of this game may be played. Teams compete against each other to see which team can hit the balloon back and forth for the longest period of time.

🔆 This game may be played indoors.

SKILLS DEVELOPED: *Ballooney* is a physical game that stimulates gross motor skills and hand-eye coordination. Because it is a team game in which all the players work together to keep the balloon off the ground, it also teaches kids about teamwork and cooperation. Counting each successful hit and comparing the number to counts from previous rounds is a lesson in problem solving as well as a way to make the game more fun and engaging.

FOLLOW ME

PURPOSE: To use visual observation skills, sequencing skills, and gross motor skills to add a link to a physical chain.

MATERIALS NEEDED: None

NUMBER OF PLAYERS: 2 or more

HOW TO PLAY: The first player goes over to an object and touches it. The next player also touches that object, then walks over to another object and touches it, too. The next player touches the two previous objects in order, then touches a third. Play continues with each player adding an object to the chain. The chain is broken when a player doesn't touch all the objects in the right sequence, or leaves one out. Move to a different area of the house or yard and start another round.

EXAMPLE: Richard, Jeff, and Sierra play *Follow Me* at a playground. Richard goes first, touching the slide. Jeff touches the slide and then the ladder. Sierra touches the slide, the ladder, and then a swing. Richard touches the slide, the ladder, the swing, and then the sandbox. Jeff touches the slide, the ladder, the swing, the sandbox, and then a toy truck. Sierra touches the slide, the ladder, the swing, the sandbox, the toy truck, and then the tunnel. Richard touches the slide, the ladder, the swing, the sandbox, and the tunnel. Sierra points out that he did not touch the toy truck. They start a new round in a different section of the playground, and Sierra goes first.

HINTS AND VARIATIONS

- 💡 Move the game to a new area for each round to prevent confusion over objects that were touched in the current round versus the previous round.
- 💡 The player who catches another player touching objects in an incorrect sequence may begin the next round.
- 💡 Play this game in a large, open area and encourage players to select objects that are at a distance from each other.
- 💡 Add a twist by requiring players to run, hop, or skip from each object to the next. The player adding a new object to the chain also selects the method of travel to that object. The other players must correctly repeat this action when they take their turns.

SKILLS DEVELOPED: *Follow Me* requires concentration and short-term memory. Players must concentrate to recall the proper sequence when they are taking their turn, and they must concentrate when they watch other players take their turns. This exercises visual observation skills and sequencing, a type of problem-solving skill. This game is also somewhat physical, as players must move across large spaces to touch objects in the correct order.

SCAVENGER HUNT

PURPOSE: To read a pictorial list and think critically about how to gather the items on the list.

MATERIALS NEEDED: Paper, pencil or crayon (one for each player), bag (one for each player)

NUMBER OF PLAYERS: 1 or more

HOW TO PLAY: Make a list of small objects that can be found in your house, yard, or immediate area, such as a rock, a leaf, an acorn, and a stick. For prereaders, use hand-drawn pictures for each item instead of words. Give each player an identical list and a bag. Review the list with the players to be sure they understand each drawing, then send them off to collect all the items on the list. Set boundaries. If there are four or more players, divide them into pairs to work together.

After finding each item, the players cross it off their lists, place it in their bags, and begin searching for the next item. Players or teams race to find every item on the list and then hand the filled bag to you. Check the bags to make sure they include the list. Rewards may be awarded to players when they filled bags.

EXAMPLE: Mom creates a scavenger hunt list for Lindsay and Nicole. She draws pictures of a leaf, an acorn, a paper clip, a piece of mail, an empty soda can, a red crayon, a pinecone, a blade of grass, a tissue, and a penny. She writes a word to label each picture. She gives the girls one bag, sets the boundaries, sets a timer, and tells them they have fifteen minutes to find everything on the list.

Lindsay and Nicole work together to find the items on the list and place them in the bag. They check the items off the list as they are found. After ten minutes, they have found everything except an empty soda can and a pinecone. They ask Mom for some hints and tips, and she directs them to certain areas of the house and yard. Just before the timer goes off, the girls find the last item on the list.

HINTS AND VARIATIONS

- Your hand-drawn pictures need not be perfect or even obvious. Just review the list with the players ahead of time and explain what each picture is.
- Consider creating your list on a computer using clip art.
- You may give each team or each player a slightly different list.
- All the players may work together as one team to find the items on the list rather than race against each other.
- Set a time limit and use a timer, or leave the end of this game open-ended, letting the search continue until all the items have been found.

SKILLS DEVELOPED: Working with lists may be new to your pre-schooler. The idea of "reading" the pictures on the list, searching for them, and checking them off is fun for children. Using lists makes kids feel grown-up because lists are often an adult activity. To add to the appeal, children are also given freedom to roam a designated area to search for particular items.

The thinking processes stimulated in this game are problem-solving skills, as children must think creatively about where to find the items on the list, and visual observation, as children must search the house or yard to find them.

STEP COUNTER

PURPOSE: To teach about measurement and stimulate spatial abilities and problem-solving skills by comparing spaces.

MATERIALS NEEDED: Paper and pencil

NUMBER OF PLAYERS: 1 or more

HOW TO PLAY: Pose a question to the players that asks which of two distances is longer. For example, which is larger, the width of the driveway or the length of the swing set? Players hypothesize the answer, then test their hypothesis by measuring the two distances in terms of paces. Each player walks the two distances, counting the number of steps he takes, and then compares the two measurements and declares which space is larger. Play several rounds.

EXAMPLE: Stella, Montana, Alexander, and Dad are playing outside. Dad asks the players which is larger, the distance between their mailbox and their neighbor's mailbox, or the distance between the two oak trees in the front yard. Stella hypothesizes that the mailbox distance is greater, while Montana and Alexander choose the tree distance. The kids each pace off the distance between the objects. For

Stella, there are twenty-one paces between the two mailboxes. Montana gets twenty-five, and Alexander gets sixteen. Dad notes each of these measurements on a piece of paper. Then they move to the oak trees. Stella measures twenty-eight paces between the two trees. Montana comes up with thirty-one, and Alexander gets eighteen. Dad reviews the measurements with each child, and they conclude that Montana's and Alexander's hypothesis is correct; the distance between the two oak trees is greater.

Dad asks for suggestions for the next round. Montana suggests measuring the width of the driveway, and Stella suggests measuring the length of the car. Again, each player hypothesizes which measurement is longer, and then actual results are compared to the predictions.

HINTS AND VARIATIONS

- In the first round, use an obvious comparison to bolster confidence.
- For advanced players, compare the distance between three objects instead of two. Or, after the longer distance has been identified, ask the players to compare that one to a third distance.
- It is recommended that an adult write down the number of paces that children count and then review the chart as a group after the game. A bar graph may be created using the data.
- After the first few rounds, involve the children in selecting the distances to be compared.
- This game may be played indoors. Rather than measuring distances in paces, measure in feet or yards.

SKILLS DEVELOPED: This game stimulates spatial thinking, as children use their visual observation skills to assess the distance between two objects and compare this distance. This comparison also involves problem-solving skills. This is a very complex game for preschoolers, who are often unable to compare large distances on sight alone.

The pacing activity teaches kids the concept of measurement and how to translate space into a concrete number. The pacing required for measuring the spaces also uses gross motor skills.

SPOON RACE

PURPOSE: To exercise gross motor skills, hand-eye coordination, and fine motor skills by balancing objects on a spoon.

MATERIALS NEEDED: Spoons, one for each player; objects to balance, such as a golf ball, Ping-Pong ball, or jelly bean

NUMBER OF PLAYERS: 2 or more

HOW TO PLAY: Establish a starting line and a finish line. Players each stand at the starting line holding a spoon with an object balanced on it. At "Go!" the players race by walking quickly (no running!) to the finish line while holding the spoon out in front of them. They must balance the object on the spoon without dropping it. If a player drops the object, she must return to the starting line. The winner assigns objects to racers in the next round.

EXAMPLE: Dad, Andrew, and Casey each line up at the starting line. Dad balances a Ping-Pong ball on his spoon, Casey balances a tennis ball, and Andrew balances a jelly bean. Andrew gets a head start, and all three players walk the length of their backyard while carrying their objects on their spoons. Dad drops the Ping-Pong ball and returns to the starting line to begin again. Casey is caught running, so she also must go back to the starting line. Andrew is the first to cross the finish line. He assigns objects to each player for the next race: Andrew gets a jelly bean again, Dad gets an egg, and Casey gets a tangerine.

HINTS AND VARIATIONS

- 🔆 Experiment with balancing different objects such as eggs (hard-boiled or uncooked), oranges and other fruits, different balls, and coins. As a group, draw conclusions about how difficult or easy it is to balance each object and discuss why.

- 🔆 To even the odds, advanced players may balance the difficult objects. Younger players may be given a head start.

- 🔆 Before starting this game, the players may set up an obstacle course to race through while balancing their objects. The obstacle course may consist of trashcans, chairs, rakes, and other objects.

- 🔆 *Spoon Race* may also be played in the shallow end of a pool.

- 🔆 If there are six or more players, this game may be played as a relay race.

- 🔆 If you decide to prohibit players from running, enforce this by requiring any runners to return to the starting line.

SKILLS DEVELOPED: *Spoon Race* requires players to move quickly while exercising physical control. They must keep themselves from running, and they must hold the spoon carefully so that their object does not drop, all while racing the other players. Give the less advanced players an advantage or a head start so they don't become frustrated. This game is more fun and challenging with an even playing field.

Manual dexterity, visual observation, and hand-eye coordination are exercised as players hold and watch their spoons to prevent their objects from falling. Gross motor skills also come into play as children walk as quickly as they can without running.

STATUES

PURPOSE: To use gross motor skills in this physical game.

MATERIALS NEEDED: None

NUMBER OF PLAYERS: 3 or more

HOW TO PLAY: An adult is the first spinner. The spinner holds the hand of the first player, spins that player around in a circle, and then lets go. The player must freeze in place like a statue. Then the spinner spins the next player, who also freezes when released.

When all the players have been spun and frozen into statues, the spinner walks from player to player, cracking jokes, making funny sounds, and trying to make the statues laugh or move. If a player moves or laughs, he is out. That player then helps the spinner try to make the remaining statues move. The last player to move becomes the spinner in the next round.

EXAMPLE: Dad holds Beth's hand, spinning around and letting go. She freezes with one leg up in the air. Then Dad spins Audrey, Will, and Despina, who also freeze in place. Dad walks from player to player, giggling and making jokes and funny faces. Eventually Audrey laughs. Audrey helps Dad by acting silly in front of Despina, who moves an arm. Despina and Audrey try to get Will to move while Dad works on Beth. Finally, Will bursts out laughing. Beth is the last player to stand frozen, so she wins the round. Beth is the spinner in the next round.

HINTS AND VARIATIONS

- Play this game in a large, open area with plenty of space and few objects for spinning players to bump into.

-ᵠ- Encourage the spinners to be gentle as they let loose the other players.

-ᵠ- Set a "no touching" rule for the spinner when he is trying to make the statues move or laugh.

-ᵠ- The more the merrier! Play this game with several players to make it even more fun.

SKILLS DEVELOPED: This physical game exercises gross motor skills by requiring players to stand frozen in unusual positions for several minutes. Preschoolers will enjoy playing this game over and over.

REVERSE HIDE-AND-SEEK

PURPOSE: To use visual observation skills and gross motor skills in this twist on a classic game.

MATERIALS NEEDED: None

NUMBER OF PLAYERS: 3 or more

HOW TO PLAY: In this game, players try to find one hidden person instead of the other way around. First, establish an area in which to hide. One player is chosen to hide. The others close their eyes and count to twenty while that player hides within the designated area. Each player goes off in search of the hider. The first seeker to find the hider calls out "Found you!" and becomes the hider in the next round.

EXAMPLE: Dylan, Bobby, Sam, and Dad play reverse hide-and-seek in their backyard. Sam is the first hider. Dylan, Bobby, and Dad lean against the house, close their eyes, and count to twenty while Sam hides. Then they go in different directions to find Sam. Dylan is the first to spot Sam, and she calls out "Found you!" Now Dylan hides while the others count to twenty.

HINTS AND VARIATIONS

- ☀️ Play this game in a large area (such as a yard) with plenty of hiding spaces.
- ☀️ Be sure all players understand the boundaries of the designated area.
- ☀️ The more the merrier! The fun is enhanced when there are several players seeking the hider.

SKILLS DEVELOPED: Children love to play this game for long periods of time. When it's played in a large area, it exercises gross motor skills as players cover lots of ground while hiding and searching. Visual observation skills are also used as players search for the hider.

ON-THE-GO
GAMES

ALPHABET SPOTTING

PURPOSE: To sharpen visual observation skills and knowledge of beginning letter sounds.

MATERIALS NEEDED: None

NUMBER OF PLAYERS: 2 or more

HOW TO PLAY: This game can be played while seated in a room or at a table in a restaurant. The first player looks around the room to find an object that begins with the letter A. Once she's spotted one, she says the word aloud. The next player searches for another object that begins with the letter A and announces the object he finds. Play continues until one player can't identify an object that starts with the designated letter. Then the next round begins, starting with the last player to find an object in the previous round. That player tries to find an object that begins with the letter B. This round continues until no more objects are found, then the group moves on to the letter C. Continue through as many alphabet letters as possible.

EXAMPLE: While they are waiting for their food at a restaurant, Mom, Dad, Leo, and Cala play *Alphabet Spotting*. These are the objects they spot that begin with the letter A: Mom: apple pie. Leo: arm. Cala: Alexandra, their server. Dad: arrow. Mom: art. Leo: aluminum foil. Cala: ankle. Dad: angelic children. Mom: apparel. Leo: arch. Cala: aquarium. Dad: arrangement of flowers. Mom: automobile in a picture on the wall.

When it is Leo's turn, he is stumped. The group moves on to the letter B, and Mom names the first word since she was the last player to find a word that begins with the letter A. After identifying several words that begin with the letter B, they move on to the letter C. Before they get to the letter D, their dinners arrive, and they end their game.

HINTS AND VARIATIONS

- If you play this game frequently, you may start in the middle of the alphabet once in a while so that you're not always beginning with the letter A. The first player may pick the starting letter.
- Encourage the use of creative words. Players may use colors and adjectives that begin with the designated letter. For example, for the letter L, acceptable answers may include "lavender purse," "leaning tray," or "lemon scent."
- For advanced players, incorporate a provision for bluffing. Players may bluff and call out a word with the designated letter even though they haven't actually spotted that object in the room. If another player calls their bluff, that player wins the round. If one player accuses another player of bluffing when he hasn't, then the wrongly accused player wins the round.
- Use this game as an opportunity to introduce new vocabulary words to your children.
- Take your time and play this game at a relaxed pace.
- If a player identifies an object that doesn't begin with the correct letter, give the player another chance.

SKILLS DEVELOPED: This challenging game builds vocabulary and sharpens visual observation and problem-solving skills. It also teaches and reinforces beginning letter sounds. This game is enjoyable for children of all ages.

I'M THINKING

PURPOSE: To use problem solving, listening, imagination, and language skills to identify an animal that has been selected by another player.

MATERIALS NEEDED: None

NUMBER OF PLAYERS: 2 or more

HOW TO PLAY: The youngest player is "it" first. "It" selects an animal and says, "I'm thinking of an animal." Rotating around the group, the other players try to guess which animal "it" has in mind. First, they ask "it" one question to help identify the animal. Then, after the question is answered, they can name the animal. If the guess is incorrect, the next player takes a turn. The player who guesses correctly is "it" in the next round.

EXAMPLE: Mom, Johnny, and Amy are waiting at the doctor's office. Johnny is the youngest, so he is "it" first. Johnny thinks of a giraffe. He says, "I'm thinking of an animal."

Amy asks, "Is the animal bigger or smaller than our dog?" Johnny says it is bigger. Amy guesses, "Is it an elephant?" Johnny answers no.

Mom asks, "How many legs does the animal have?" Johnny says four. Mom guesses, "Is it a polar bear?" Johnny says no again.

Amy asks, "Does the animal have stripes?" Johnny shakes his head. Amy asks if it is a leopard, but she is incorrect.

Mom asks, "Is the animal in the zoo?" Johnny nods. Mom asks if it is a rhinoceros and Johnny says no.

Amy asks, "Does the animal have a long neck?" Johnny says yes. Amy correctly guesses, "Is the animal a giraffe?"

Now Amy thinks of a snake. "I'm thinking of an animal," she says. Is the animal extinct?" Mom asks. Amy says no. "Does the animal have fur?" Johnny asks. "No," answers Amy. The game continues until someone guesses Amy's animal. Then it becomes that player's turn.

HINTS AND VARIATIONS

- Young players may appreciate a more free-flowing game in which participants ask questions and guess at random. This may be a good way to introduce the game.

☀ This game may be turned into a version of the traditional *Twenty Questions* game by requiring each player to ask only a yes or no question and by limiting the number of questions to twenty. These rules make the game more difficult.

☀ You may set a rule that if any player asks a "repeat question,"—a question that's already been posed by another player in that round—he loses his chance to guess an animal on that turn.

☀ Instead of animals, think of people, characters, foods, books, or toys.

☀ After each animal has been identified, share information about that animal, such as its predators or its prey, where they live, and what their young look like.

☀ When you get home, ask each child to draw a picture of one of the animals from the game.

SKILLS DEVELOPED: Problem-solving skills are stimulated in this game when your child asks questions to help identify the selected animal. One of the most challenging aspects of this game is to use the information from previous questions to figure out which animal fits the description. Language skills are exercised as children ask questions, and general knowledge about animals increases. Children enjoy being "it" and using their imagination to select an animal that will be challenging for the others to guess.

BOX BLOCKS

PURPOSE: To learn to think critically and strategically.

MATERIALS NEEDED: Paper; pencil, pen, crayon, or marker

NUMBER OF PLAYERS: 2 or more

HOW TO PLAY: Make several rows of dots on a piece of paper, creating a grid of dots. The first player connects two dots by drawing a line from one dot to another. The second player does the same. Each player takes a turn connecting two dots. The object is to be the person whose line completes a box. Once a player has drawn a line that completes a box, the player writes his initials inside the box. Continue playing until the grid is filled with boxes. Then each player counts the number of boxes with her initials. The player with the highest count wins.

EXAMPLE: While they are waiting for their food to be served at a restaurant, Mom, Dad, Michael, and Erica play *Box Blocks.* Mom creates a grid by drawing six rows of six evenly spaced dots on the back of a paper place mat. Michael goes first, connecting two dots together. Next, Erica connects two dots, then Mom, and finally Dad. No one has completed a box. Michael draws a line that completes a box. He writes an M inside the box. Erica connects two more dots. The foursome continue connecting dots and completing boxes until most of the grid is filled. Then the players count up the number of boxes with their initials inside them.

HINTS AND VARIATIONS

- It is not necessary to complete all the boxes in the grid. This game can be played while the group is waiting for something, such as a meal to be served. When the meal arrives, play ends.
- You may play *Reverse Box Blocks,* where each player tries *not* to draw the last line to enclose a box. The player with the lowest score wins.

SKILLS DEVELOPED: When preschoolers first play *Box Blocks,* they are likely to enjoy drawing random lines and may be surprised (and delighted) when their line completes a box. In time, though, they learn to recognize "box opportunities," or boxes with three sides that need one more line to complete. Begin to point these out to new players after they've grown accustomed to the basics of the game. Eventually, players may even learn to play defensively and be careful not to create "box opportunities" for other players.

Over time, *Box Blocks* teaches children to think critically and strategically. They must use visual observation skills to scan the grid for "box opportunities" each turn, and they must use problem-solving skills to count the number of blocks labeled with their initials at the end of the game.

🛒 RAINBOW SHOPPING

PURPOSE: To sharpen observation and language skills in this grocery store game.

MATERIALS NEEDED: Squeaky toy

NUMBER OF PLAYERS: 2 or more

HOW TO PLAY: Bring the squeaky toy on your next trip to the grocery store. On the way, each player selects a color. Inside the store, whenever a player spots a food or other object in her color, she calls it out. She squeaks the toy and keeps it until another player identifies a food. That player calls it out, takes the toy, and squeaks it. The toy is passed back and forth between players as each one identifies a food in his color.

EXAMPLE: Mom, Calvin, and Gwen each pick a color on the way to the grocery store. Mom chooses green, Calvin red, and Gwen yellow. The squeaky toy is placed in the seat of the shopping cart.

Gwen spots bananas right away and calls out "Bananas!" She reaches for the squeaky toy and squeezes it. She holds it until Mom says "Broccoli!" Mom squeaks the toy and keeps it. When Calvin says "Apples!," he squeaks the toy. As they go through the store, they take turns calling out food in their designated color, and passing and squeaking the toy.

HINTS AND VARIATIONS

- Instead of colors, this game can be played with letters of the alphabet. Each player selects a letter and looks for foods that begin with that letter. Players may also use the first letter of their name.

- The squeaky toy is not necessary, but it adds an element of fun. Preschoolers seem to enjoy holding the squeaky toy while other players are searching for a food in their color or letter, and they are disappointed when the toy is taken from them.

- Set a rule that if there is any fighting over the toy, the game ends.

- This game can be played in stores other than grocery stores.

SKILLS DEVELOPED: *Rainbow Shopping* makes a mundane activity like grocery shopping more fun. Children will look at the grocery store through new eyes. They sharpen their visual observation skills as they search the store for objects in the right color or beginning with the right letter. This game also reinforces and teaches beginning word sounds. Children may even learn to identify new foods.

GAME
OVERVIEWS

CAR GAMES

HIPPOPOTAMUS. Players think of a sentence that describes a true fact about one or more of the other players, then substitute the word *hippopotamus* for a noun in the sentence. The other players try to guess the correct word. (Problem solving, auditory observation, imagination, language and expression.)

PEOPLE STORIES. In the car, the youngest player points out a stranger and begins to create a story about that person. The next person picks up where the first player left off, adding details to the story. The storytelling rotates around the car, giving everyone a chance to add to the story. (Visual observation, imagination, language and expression.)

SALT AND PEPPER. In the car, one player is designated Salt and the other is designated Pepper. Salt looks for white cars and Pepper looks for black cars. Every time Salt spots a white car, he calls out "Salt!" Every time Pepper spots a black car, he calls out "Pepper!" Players keep count of how many cars they spot. (Visual observation, problem solving.)

ALPHABET ONE, TWO, THREE. Players look outside the car for objects or words that begin with the selected letter, starting with A. When a player spots a word that begins with the selected letter, she calls it out. Each player counts how many objects or words he has spotted, and play continues until one player has found and called out three objects or words that begin with the selected letter. (Visual observation, problem solving.)

OPPOSITES. An adult says a word and players respond with its opposite. (Problem solving, auditory observation, language and expression.)

RHYMIN' SIMON. In the first round, an adult or other older player selects a starting word. Rotating around the car, players take turns naming words that rhyme with the starting word. If a player can't think of a word, she may skip her turn. The round ends when players cannot think of another rhyming word. The last player to think of a rhyming word selects a word for the next round. (Problem solving, auditory observation, language and expression.)

LICENSE PLATE COUNTING. Players work as a team to count from one to nine by spotting these digits on license plates. Play rotates around the car as players take turns finding the next number. The first player searches for a one, the next player looks for a two, and so on, until all digits from one to nine have been found in order. (Visual observation, problem solving.)

LICENSE PLATE NAME GAME. Players work as a team to spell the name of a person in the car. Players search for the letters on license plates, calling out the letters in the correct order as they are spotted. The player who spots the last letter of the selected name is honored by having his name spelled in the next round. (Visual observation, problem solving.)

ANALOGIES. A player selects a food. All the players think of a non-food object that the food reminds them of. The players take turns revealing their analogy and explaining why it reminds them of the food selected. (Problem solving, auditory observation, imagination, language and expression.)

THESAURUS. An adult says the starting word, and the first player responds by saying a synonym for the starting word. The other players think of additional synonyms, one player at a time, in a rotating fashion. (Problem solving, auditory observation, language and expression.)

IMAGINARY PIZZA. The first player begins by saying, "I'm going to top my imaginary pizza with cheese." The next player repeats the sentence and adds another topping. The next player repeats the previous player's sentence and adds her own topping. Play continues until one player cannot recall all the previous toppings. Then a new round is started by the last player to name all the pizza toppings in the previous round. (Auditory observation, memory, imagination, language and expression.)

WORD CHAINS. The first player begins by saying a word out loud. The second player calls out a word that begins with the letter that the previous word ends with. The third player calls out a word that begins with the letter that the second player's word ends with. The word chain grows as play continues around the car. Words may not be repeated. When a player gets stumped, the round ends. The last player to add a word to the word chain starts the next round with a new word. (Problem solving, auditory observation, language and expression.)

LACE RACE. Before a car trip, simple lacing boards are created by cutting basic shapes such as a star or a house out of a piece of cardboard or poster board and punching several holes in the shape. The holes are numbered in one sequence on one side, then numbered on the other side in a different sequence. Long pieces of yarn are cut; one end is taped to the center of each lacing board. During the car ride, each player gets a lacing board. They must thread the yarn in and out of the holes on the board, following the sequence prescribed by the numbers written next to each hole. (Problem solving, motor skills.)

SPONTANEOUS. The first player says any word out loud. The next player responds by saying a word that comes to mind when he hears the first word. The next player must say a word that relates to the previous word. Play continues, with each player adding a word. (Problem solving, auditory observation, imagination, language and expression.)

LIST MAKER. Players prepare for a car trip by developing a list of objects they expect to see from the car window. The items on the list may be hand-drawn pictures, stickers, or words. Players draw a small box next to each picture. On the road trip, as the child spots an item on the list, she calls it out and checks it off. (Visual observation, problem solving, imagination, language and expression, artistic expression.)

APPLES FOR MY TEACHER. The first player selects a number from one to five as the starting number and says she will give her teacher that number of apples. The next player tells how many apples he will give to the teacher and the total number of apples that the teacher will now have. Each player continues giving the teacher more apples (always a number between one and five) until the teacher has more than twenty apples. (Problem solving, auditory observation.)

CRAZY EIGHTS. An adult selects a number from one to eight and says, "I have X pennies in my pile but I wish I had eight," substituting the chosen number for X. The first player states how many pennies must be added to the adult's pile in order for the adult to have eight pennies. Then the adult selects a new number from one to eight and says it aloud in the same sentence for the next player. That player states how many pennies must be added to the pile in order for the adult to have eight pennies. (Problem solving, auditory observation.)

HI, MY NAME IS ALICE. Play rotates around the car, with the first player creating a description of a person based on the letter A, the second player based on the letter B, the third player C, and so on. On his turn, each player completes the following sentence: "Hi, my name is _____ and my brother's (or sister's) name is _____. We come from _____ and we sell _____." Each blank must be filled in with a word beginning with the appropriate letter. (Problem solving, auditory observation, imagination, language and expression.)

ROADSIDE CRIBBAGE. The Left Team (left side of the car) and the Right Team (right side of the car) search outside the car for objects from a predetermined list (such as cows, trucks, police cars) and earn points for their team based on how many objects they spot on their side of the road. (Visual observation, problem solving.)

NAME THAT TUNE. An adult plays the first few seconds of a familiar children's song on a CD and then pauses it. Players who know the song title are asked to call it out. If no one can name the title, a few more seconds of the song are played, and players are given another chance to name that tune. (Problem solving, auditory observation.)

NAME THAT SOUND. Before a road trip or gathering, one child uses a cassette recorder to record common household and outdoor sounds with the help of an adult. On the road trip, the cassette is played, and the other players try to guess the source of each sound. (Problem solving, auditory observation, artistic expression.)

SONGWRITER. An adult chooses a song to be rewritten, such as "Twinkle, Twinkle, Little Star." Players take turns rewriting selected rhyming lines from the song. (Problem solving, auditory observation, language and expression.)

HOME GAMES

TREASURE HUNT. An adult draws a map or floor plan of the house and explains it to the players. While the other players turn their backs, the adult hides a particular toy in one room of the house. Then the adult posts the map on the refrigerator using magnets. The adult places one magnet on the map to indicate the location of the hidden toy. Using the map, the players try to find the toy. The first player to find the toy hides it in the next round and places the magnet on the map. (Visual observation, spatial ability, imagination.)

PHOTO CONCENTRATION. Players take photographs of at least six different subjects of their choosing. The film is developed and double prints are obtained. Players select six or more photos along with their duplicates. The photos are shuffled and laid facedown on a flat surface. The players take turns turning over two photos. If the photos match, the player keeps those two photos and takes another turn. If they do not match, the player turns the photos facedown again, and the next player takes a turn. Play continues until all the photos have been matched. Each player counts the number of photos she collected during the game. (Visual observation, problem solving, memory, artistic expression, motor skills.)

M&M SUBTRACTION. Start with ten M&Ms on a table. An inverted mug is placed next to the M&Ms. The first player counts the M&Ms. Then he closes his eyes while an adult puts a few of the M&Ms under the mug. When he opens his eyes, he guesses how many M&Ms are under the mug based on the number of M&Ms that are outside the mug. When he guesses correctly, he may eat the M&Ms under the mug. Then the next player takes a turn. Continue playing until no candies are left. (Visual observation, problem solving.)

SECRET BOX. The Box Keeper selects a household object, discreetly places it inside the Secret Box and closes the box cover. The Box Keeper tells the other players the first letter of the object in the Secret Box. The other players take turns guessing what's in the box. The first player to guess correctly becomes the Box Keeper in the next round. (Spatial ability, language and expression.)

COLOR MAKERS. Each player closes her eyes and selects a crayon from a bowl. Players are then given clear bottles half-filled with water and a set of liquid food coloring. Players drop the food coloring into their bottle to tint the water to match the color of the crayon they selected. (Visual observation, problem solving, experimentation, artistic expression.)

DINNERTIME! At mealtime, one family member is designated as the cashier, who then sets a price for each food served in the meal. As the food is served, the cashier announces the price for each item and the players set aside play money to pay for it. At the end of the meal, the players must add up the cost of what they ate and pay the cashier. (Problem solving, auditory observation.)

NEWSPAPER NUMBERS. Players search the newspaper for the numbers one through ten. As they find the numbers, they cut them out and arrange them on a blank piece of paper in order from lowest to highest. (Visual observation, problem solving, motor skills.)

HOME PHONE. For each player, a set of seven cards is created with one digit on each card. Collectively, the set of seven cards makes up the player's home phone number. Each player shuffles her cards. Each player must lay his cards out on a flat surface and then rearrange them until they are in the order of his home phone number. (Visual observation, problem solving, memory, motor skills.)

THE COVER-UP. The numbers one through six are written on each player's blank piece of paper. The first player rolls two dice, calls out the numbers he rolled, and places a penny over each of the corresponding numbers on his paper. The next player takes her turn, and play continues until one player has covered all the numbers on his paper with pennies. (Visual observation, problem solving, motor skills.)

MEASURING UP. First, the players are given a lesson on how to take measurements using a ruler, tape measure, or yardstick. Then an adult selects one object for each player to measure. Players measure their objects and compare their measurements to determine whose object is taller, wider, or deeper. (Visual observation, problem solving, spatial ability, motor skills.)

DICE ROUNDS. Players take turns rolling two dice. Each player adds up the numbers on the face of the dice and announces the sum. After all players have rolled the dice, the group determines who had the highest roll. That player wins a penny or a poker chip and is the first to roll the dice in the next round. Play for several rounds, and declare a winner based on who has collected the highest number of pennies or poker chips. (Problem solving, visual observation.)

SKYSCRAPERS. A box of small paper cups is divided evenly among the players or teams. Send the teams to different rooms and ask each team to build the highest possible structure by stacking the cups on top of one another in a creative way within ten minutes. (Problem solving, visual observation, motor skills, spatial ability, experimentation.)

VIRTUAL SHOPPING. Players flip through magazines and catalogs, identify things they like, and cut them out. They glue their cutouts to a piece of paper to create their own one-page catalog of favorite items. Then they set a dollar price for each item and write the number underneath each picture. (Visual observation, problem solving, motor skills.)

GRAPHIC CLOTHES. A bar chart is made using a piece of paper with the days of the week along the bottom of the chart and the numbers one through twelve up the left side. An adult posts this chart in the child's bedroom. Each morning before the child gets dressed, the adult asks her how many pieces of clothing she thinks she'll be wearing that day. Then, as she gets dressed, she counts the number of articles of clothing that she's putting on and compares this to her prediction. Together, adult and child record the number of clothing pieces on the chart by creating a shaded bar for the current day. The child can help by coloring the bar with markers or crayons. Each subsequent day, compare numbers to past days. (Problem solving, spatial ability.)

SHAPE MAKING. Players receive several toothpicks each, and each player arranges his toothpicks into two shapes, three shapes, or four shapes. Each player may have a different number of starting toothpicks. Once all players have created the shapes, review the names of the shapes. (Problem solving, experimentation, spatial ability, motor skills.)

SHAPE HUNT. With an adult's help, the children first cut several shapes out of paper, such as a circle, square, rectangle, triangle, and oval. These shapes are put into a bowl, and players blindly draw one out. Players flip through magazines hunting for pictures or drawings that are the same as the selected shape. As the shapes are spotted, players cut them out and glue them to their paper. When the paper is filled, players count the number of shapes they collected and write the total on the bottom of the page. (Visual observation, problem solving, artistic expression, motor skills.)

WHAT'S DIFFERENT? The players are sent out of the room, and an adult changes or moves one object in the room. For example, a picture frame may be turned upside down, or a stuffed animal may be seated in a chair. When the adult is finished, he calls the players back into the room. They look around, try to spot the change, and call it out once it's been identified. (Visual observation, problem solving, memory.)

DETECTIVE MEMORY. An adult places ten household objects on a large plate or tray and covers them with a cloth or towel. Players sit in a circle and the covered tray is placed in the middle of the circle. The adult removes the cover and asks the players to name all the objects they see on the tray. The adult then removes the tray and asks the players to name the objects that were on it. The adult writes down the objects that are recalled and gives clues for the objects that are not recalled. The adult then brings the tray back and asks the group to identify the objects they forgot. (Visual observation, problem solving, memory.)

HUCKLE BUCKLE BEANSTALK. In each round, one child plays the role of the hider and all the other players are the finders. The finders leave the designated room. Without moving any objects, the hider hides a small toy in a location that is visible yet not too obvious. The finders must keep their hands behind their backs as they search for the hidden toy. They cannot touch or move anything as they look for it. When the toy is spotted by a player, she calls out, "Huckle Buckle Beanstalk!" In the next round, that player is the hider. (Visual observation, problem solving.)

MENU MAKER. Players cut out pictures of their favorite foods and glue them to a folded piece of paper to create a menu. They write labels and prices under each photo and pretend to order food from the menu. They receive and pay the bill using play money. (Visual observation, problem solving, imagination, motor skills.)

TASTE TEST. Players close their eyes and pop a flavored jelly bean into their mouths. Players remain silent while everyone chews the jelly bean. On the count of three, players call out their guesses as to their jelly bean's flavor. (Nonvisual observation.)

SNIFF TEST. An adult places several items with pungent smells into small paper cups and covers them with pieces of cheesecloth. Players sniff each cup and try to identify the smells. An adult records guesses on an answer sheet. The cheesecloth covers are removed and the contents of the cups are revealed. Guesses are compared with the actual items. (Nonvisual observation.)

TOUCH POINTS. Five to ten objects with unique textures or shapes are gathered and placed one at a time into an empty tissue box. Players take turns reaching into the box to touch the object. Once everyone's had a chance to feel the object, an adult counts to three and all players simultaneously call out their guesses as to what the object is. The adult takes out the object to show all the players, and they compare their guesses to the actual object. (Nonvisual observation.)

FREEZE-FRAME. An adult plays music and the players dance. When the volume is turned up loud, players dance rapidly, and when the volume is turned down low, players dance slowly. When the music stops, the players must freeze in place. Players try to hold their freeze position as long as possible. The last player to move wins the round. (Nonvisual observation, artistic expression, motor skills.)

HAND PUZZLE. Players trace the outline of their hand on heavyweight paper or cardboard, color it in, and cut it out. Then they cut the hand itself into several small puzzle pieces. The pieces are shuffled and the players reassemble their hand by putting the pieces back together. (Visual observation, problem solving, artistic expression, motor skills.)

MISSING LETTERS. Magnetic letters are used to spell out a word with one letter missing. An adult writes the entire word on a piece of paper. Players find the missing magnetic letter and put it in place. (Visual observation, problem solving.)

HIGH CARD. The face cards and aces are removed from a deck of cards. The remaining cards are dealt evenly among the players. Players stack their cards facedown in front of them. Each player turns over one card, and the player with the highest card wins all the cards that have been turned over in that round. However, if a player turns over a card with a number that is equal to his age, then he wins that card. After all cards have been played, the players count the number of cards they won. (Visual observation, problem solving.)

CARNIVAL TOSS. An adult sets up beanbag targets by arranging bowls, pie plates, and pans on the floor and assigning a value of one, two, or three points to each target. Each player is given three beanbags. Players stand behind a yardstick and try to toss their beanbags into the targets. At the end of their turn, players count the points they have earned and receive one penny for every point. Once all players have taken their turn, players compare points. (Visual observation, problem solving, motor skills.)

NUMBER PUZZLES. Numbers are written on the top half of twelve small pieces of construction paper. Players draw the corresponding number of objects on the bottom of each paper. Each piece is cut in half, so that the number is on one half and the drawings are on the other. The pieces are shuffled and laid out. Players take turns selecting a number from the top row and finding the matching drawing. If they are successful, they keep both pieces. If they are not, they return the pieces and the next player takes his turn. Once all numbers have been selected and matched, players count the number of pieces of paper each has. (Visual observation, problem solving, artistic expression.)

ALPHABET DRAWINGS. Players brainstorm as many words as they can that begin with a selected letter of the alphabet. Then players have ten minutes to draw five or more pictures of words that begin with the designated letter. (Imagination, language and expression, artistic expression.)

DOMINO CONTEST. A set of dominoes is laid out facedown. Each player selects one domino. Players take turns revealing their dominoes, naming the number of dots on each side and naming the sum of all the dots. The player with the most dots wins the round and collects all the dominoes. After all the facedown dominoes are gone, players count their dominoes. (Visual observation, problem solving.)

MONEY HUNT. One player hides pennies and nickels on windowsills around the house. The other players race from room to room to find the money. They trade in their nickels for five pennies each, then count the total number of pennies they collected. The player with the most money wins and hides the coins for the next round. (Visual observation, problem solving.)

BEANBAG BALANCE. A starting line and a finish line are established. The first player balances a beanbag anywhere on her body as she makes her way from the starting line to the finish line. She may travel in any manner she chooses, such as hop, skip, walk, or crawl. The goal is to make it to the finish line without dropping the beanbag. The other players must follow the first player's challenge and carry their beanbags from start to finish in the same manner as the first player. (Visual observation, imagination, motor skills.)

PICKUP STICKS. Twenty or more toothpicks are dumped onto a table. Players take turns trying to remove one toothpick without disturbing or touching any other toothpicks. If a player is successful, he keeps that toothpick. If another toothpick moves in the process, however, he must return the toothpick back to the pile. Once all toothpicks have been removed, players count the number of toothpicks they have earned. (Visual observation, problem solving.)

TOOTHPICK ONE, TWO, THREE. Fifteen toothpicks are laid on a table. The first player takes one, two, or three toothpicks from the pile. The next player also takes one, two, or three. Continue rotating turns, with players taking one, two, or three toothpicks on each turn. The player who picks up the last toothpick loses the game. (Visual observation, problem solving.)

RATTLESNAKE. An adult gathers ten small objects that will fit inside an empty film canister, such as pasta, a cotton ball, and a paper clip. One object is placed inside the canister. The players shake the canister and try to guess what's inside based on a duplicate set of small objects. (Nonvisual observation.)

EGG CARTON RACE. Each player receives an empty egg carton and a bowl of objects to sort, such as mixed crackers, mixed nuts, Froot Loops cereal, or M&Ms. The players race to sort their objects into individual egg carton cups. (Visual observation, problem solving, motor skills.)

HOLIDAY BINGO. Players play bingo after creating their own bingo cards using heavyweight paper and stickers related to a particular holiday or special day theme. (Visual observation, auditory observation, problem solving, motor skills.)

INVENTORY. Players draw pictures of several household and clothing items that are plentiful around their house, such as socks, sweaters, spoons, and keys. Each picture is cut out and placed into a bowl or jar. Every day, a different drawing is pulled, and players must locate and count all of these objects in the house. An adult helps players create and fill in a single bar on a graph. Each day, another bar is added to the graph. Over time, players compare the inventory of items. (Visual observation, problem solving, imagination, artistic expression.)

LETTER MATCH. One set of alphabet letters is placed in a bowl, and another is set out on a flat surface. Each player selects one letter from the bowl, and then searches through the other set to find the matching letter. Once all players have found their matching letters, the first player must name three words that begin with her letter. The next player must name three words that begin with his letter. Play continues until all letters have been selected. (Visual observation, imagination, language and expression.)

TRACING GAME. Players collect several household objects or toys and trace their outlines onto paper. Then they switch papers with another player. Each player tries to match up the objects with the outlines by placing the correct object on top of each outline. (Visual observation, spatial ability, imagination, motor skills.)

PHOTO SAFARI. Photos are taken of familiar neighborhood objects such as a fire hydrant, a house, a sign, a dog, and a fence. After the photos are developed, small cards are created with a word on each one that identifies the subject of one of the photos. The photos and the word cards are arranged on a table. Players take turns selecting a photo and trying to find the matching word. (Visual observation, memory, language and expression.)

WRAP IT UP. Scraps of wrapping paper or fabric are each cut into two pieces. One half of each scrap is hidden in somewhat obvious hiding spots in one room or a few rooms. The mates are placed in a bag or bowl. Players take turns reaching into the bag for a scrap, then searching for its mate. Once a player finds a mate, she returns to the bag to draw a new scrap. Play continues until all scraps have been matched. (Visual observation, problem solving.)

PHOTO SORT. An adult gathers several different photos of each player, starting from baby photos through the child's current age, and lays the photos of one child out of sequence on a table. The first player must select the photo of the child at the youngest age and start a line. The next player must select the next youngest photo and lay it next to the first. Play continues, with each player selecting the next chronological photo and placing it in line. If a selection is incorrect, the player must return it and the next player takes his turn. (Visual observation, problem solving.)

PLACEWARES. Paper plates, napkins, and cups from past birthday and holiday occasions are saved in a box. When it's mealtime, one napkin or plate from each pattern are placed in a bowl. Each player draws one item out of the bowl and finds the accompanying pieces in the box. Players set the table with a unique set of matching plate, napkin, and cup for each person. (Visual observation, problem solving.)

RED DAY. Each day, the family draws the name of a color out of a jar to determine the color for the next day. Players brainstorm ways to incorporate this color into their day. Players keep count of all the items of this color that they use, eat, and wear throughout the day. (Visual observation, imagination.)

BLIND SHAPES. Poster board is cut into shapes, which are placed into a large sock. The name of each shape is written on a small piece of paper and placed into a bowl or jar. One at a time, players reach into the jar and select the name of a shape. Then they must reach into the sock to find that shape without looking. (Nonvisual observation.)

LETTER DOUGH. Each player closes his eyes and selects an alphabet letter. The player thinks of three words that begin with that letter as he rolls and molds clay into the shape of his letter. (Visual observation, language and expression, motor skills.)

BE A PENCIL. Players take turns pulling a picture of an inanimate object out of a bowl and use their bodies to act out that object. The other players call out guesses. The player who correctly identifies the object is the actor in the next round. (Artistic expression, motor skills.)

RAINBOW SNACK. Each player organizes twenty M&Ms into piles of unique colors. The players count the number of candies in each pile and determine which pile has the greatest number. The owner of the largest pile eats those M&Ms. Then players determine which of the remaining piles has the largest number, and that owner eats those. Continue until all the M&Ms are gone. (Visual observation, problem solving, motor skills.)

ALLIGATOR TAG. An adult lies on the floor with eyes closed. Starting from an adjacent room, players sneak up to the adult and touch her without getting caught. If the adult hears a player, she may open her eyes, "catch" the player, and send him back to the adjacent room. The first player to successfully tag the adult wins the round. (Motor skills.)

SOCK TOSS. One player is designated the target. All other players lie on the floor while the target stands facing them with arms straight down. Players take turns tossing sock balls up at the target, aiming for the hands. When a player hits a hand, she earns a point. When one player has accumulated five points, she becomes the target in the next round and the previous target lies on the floor with the other players. (Motor skills.)

DRESS-UP RACE. Each player selects an outfit to wear that day. The timer is set for five minutes. All players race to be the first one dressed. A sticker is awarded to any player who is completely dressed before the timer sounds. Place stickers on a calendar. Once a player has earned five or ten stickers, award a special prize or reward to that player. (Motor skills.)

JUMPING PENNIES. Players trace pennies on a piece of paper to create a pyramid of fifteen pennies. Each player places fourteen pennies on any fourteen of the fifteen circles on their paper. A penny may jump over an adjacent penny to land in an empty circle. After each jump, the penny that was jumped over is removed from the paper. Continue jumping pennies until no more jumps are possible. The goal is to be left with as few pennies as possible. (Visual observation, problem solving, motor skills.)

ANIMAL PANTOMIMES. The first player selects an animal and acts out the movements of that animal without making any sounds. The other players try to guess the animal. The player who correctly identifies the animal is the next performer. (Visual observation, problem solving, imagination, artistic expression, motor skills.)

❋ OUTDOOR GAMES

BALLOONEY. Players hit a balloon back and forth without letting it touch the ground. As a team, the players count aloud the number of hits they give the balloon. Players try to beat their last score. (Visual observation, problem solving, motor skills.)

FOLLOW ME. The first player walks over to an object and touches it. The next player child touches that object, goes over to another object, and touches it, too. The next player touches the two previous objects in order, then touches a third. Play continues, with each player adding an object to the chain. The chain is broken when a player doesn't touch the objects in the right sequence or leaves one out. (Visual observation, problem solving, memory, motor skills.)

SCAVENGER HUNT. An adult makes a list of small objects that can be found in the yard such as a rock, a leaf, an acorn, and a stick. For pre-readers, use hand-drawn pictures instead of words for each item on the list. Each player gets an identical list and a bag. Players must find and collect all the items on the list. (Visual observation, problem solving.)

STEP COUNTER. An adult asks the players which of two distances is larger. For example, which is larger, the width of the driveway or the length of the swing set? Players hypothesize the answer, then test their hypothesis by measuring the two distances in terms of paces. (Visual observation, problem solving, spatial ability, motor skills.)

SPOON RACE. Players stand at the starting line, each holding a spoon with an object balanced on it, such as a golf ball or a jelly bean. At "Go!" the players race each other by quickly walking, not running, to the finish line while holding the spoon out in front of them without dropping the object. (Visual observation, motor skills.)

STATUES. An adult holds the hand of the first player, spins that player around in a circle, then lets go. The player must freeze in place like a statue. Then the adult spins and releases the next player, who also freezes in an unusual position. When all the players have been spun, the adult goes from player to player, trying to make them laugh or move. The last player to "unfreeze" wins. (Motor skills.)

REVERSE HIDE-AND-SEEK. One player hides in a designated area while the others seek. The first seeker to find the hider wins and becomes the hider in the next round. (Visual observation, motor skills.)

ON-THE-GO GAMES

ALPHABET SPOTTING. The first player looks for an object that begins with the letter A. When she finds it, she calls it out. The next player searches for another object that begins with A. Play continues until a player can't identify an object that starts with the designated letter. Then the next round begins, starting with the last player to find an object in the previous round. That player finds the first object that begins with the letter B. In the next round, the letter C is used, and so forth. (Visual observation, problem solving, language and expression.)

I'M THINKING. "It" begins by saying, "I'm thinking of an animal." The other players try to guess the animal. First, they ask "it" one question to help identify the animal. Second, after the question is answered, they try to name the animal. If the guess is incorrect, it is the next player's turn. The player who correctly identifies the animal becomes "it" in the next round. (Problem solving, auditory observation, imagination, language and expression.)

BOX BLOCKS. A grid of dots is created. The first player connects two dots by drawing a line between them. The second player does the same. Each player takes a turn connecting two dots. The object is to be the one to make a line that completes a box. Once a player has done that, he writes his initial inside the box. Continue playing until the grid is filled with boxes. Then each player counts the number of boxes with her initial. (Visual observation, problem solving.)

RAINBOW SHOPPING. Each player selects a color. At the grocery store, whenever a player spots a food or other object in his color, he calls it out and squeezes a squeaky toy. He holds the toy until another player identifies a food in her color. The squeaky toy is passed back and forth between players as each identifies a food in his or her color. (Visual observation, language and expression.)

INDEX